Travelling by Train
in the Edwardian Age

'*Steam Past*' *Books from Allen & Unwin*

THE LIMITED by O. S. Nock
BIRTH OF BRITISH RAIL by Michael R. Bonavia
STEAM'S INDIAN SUMMER by George Heiron & Eric Treacy
GRAVEYARD OF STEAM by Brian Handley
PRESERVED STEAM IN BRITAIN by Patrick B. Whitehouse
TRAVELLING BY TRAIN IN THE EDWARDIAN AGE by Philip Unwin
MEN OF THE GREAT WESTERN by Peter Grafton

Travelling by Train in the Edwardian Age

Philip Unwin

London
GEORGE ALLEN & UNWIN
Boston   Sydney

First published in 1979

GEORGE ALLEN & UNWIN LTD
40 Museum Street, London WC1A 1LU

© George Allen & Unwin (Publishers) Ltd, 1979

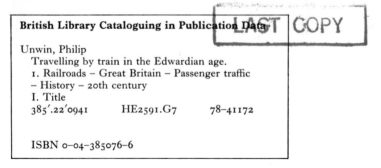

British Library Cataloguing in Publication Data

Unwin, Philip
    Travelling by train in the Edwardian age.
    1. Railroads – Great Britain – Passenger traffic
    – History – 20th century
    I. Title
    385'.22'0941   HE2591.G7   78–41172

    ISBN 0–04–385076–6

Picture research by Mike Esau.

Book designed by Design Matters/Diane Sawyer

Typeset in 11 on 12 point Imprint by Bedford Typesetters Limited and printed in Great Britain by
W. and J. Mackay Limited, Chatham.

Contents

Illustrations

Preface

It was during the reign of King Edward VII that the railways of Great Britain attained a level of speed, punctuality and comfort which was perhaps equalled but rarely excelled until many years later. The standards of that time extended to August 1914 and I make no apology for occasional references here to something which may have happened between 1910 and 1914. Essentially the aim of the book has been to recapture something of the distant but unique flavour – in sight, sound and smell – of our railways in their heyday when, for all practical purposes, the steam train was the fastest thing on earth. Seventy years ago the varying locomotive and carriage designs of over a hundred different companies gave exceptional interest and colour to the railway scene, which also reflected the social background of the times and the very different level of wages and prices.

As it is nearly sixty years since the names of the separate companies disappeared with the Grouping of 1923, the full name of each one has been given at its first mention, e.g. London and North Western Railway or Great Eastern, and subsequently it is referred to merely by its initials, LNWR or GER. An exception has been made in the case of the Midland since MR looks rather mean for so splendid a line. As the work of a Home Counties man, the book is concerned mainly with the London-based railways and it is hoped that no offence will be taken on this account by Northerners. Had I possessed Edwardian memories of such great lines as the North Eastern, with its record runs between Darlington and York, or the Lancashire and Yorkshire, with its famous 'Highflyer' Atlantics, they would have been recorded here.

Boyhood recollection, though vivid, has had to be prompted and checked – I most readily acknowledge a debt to the works of O. S. Nock, C. Hamilton Ellis, the late Dr W. A. Tuplin, Sir Peter Allen and to files of the *Railway Magazine* for 1901–1910. Also, several minor points might not have come to light without the admirable collections of the National Railway Museum at York and of the Great Western Society at Swindon. Thanks are due also to the skill with which Mike Esau carried out most thoroughly his search for the illustrations suggested, and especially to Professor Jack Simmons for his careful reading of the manuscript and for his recommendations, all of which have been incorporated.

P.U.

I
Family Journeys

To stand upon the railway station platform, early in this century, waiting for an express train to bear you away for a holiday was, for a child, a very close approach to heaven. There was anticipation so delicious as to be all but incomprehensible to the very young of today, who travel almost exclusively by car.

For a start, it was a small miracle to find that the outside porter did actually arrive on time to transport the mountain of luggage to the station, each item with its tie-on label. He was a tough individual who led a slightly shadowy existence in a corner of the station yard – half porter and half carter; he had no uniform but he wore a brass armlet fixed so tight to his sleeve that it seemed almost to be screwed to his arm and he could carry enormous trunks on his back single-handed. He would ascend to a first-floor landing bringing with him that smell of stale sweat almost inevitable for those who did hard physical work in days before their houses had bathrooms; he would get a three-decker trunk up on end and most dexterously tip it forward on to his back while he stood two or three steps down the stairs. Thus he carried it down and, by the same method in reverse, he tipped it backwards onto the tailboard of his cart. So the luggage found its way to the station and all

the vast paraphernalia of trunks, suitcases, Gladstone bags of solid leather, probably a lidded tin bath full of bathing dresses and beach clothes, plus rugs, sticks and a folding cot were then all labelled with the railway's stick-on label and assembled on the platform. This mass of baggage was quite normal for a family of modest means: even £700 a year went a long way in 1909. The party usually walked to the station.

Such a journey could begin on the middle platform at Surbiton station, which served the fast 'through' lines of the London and South Western Railway, the two outer platforms being for local trains – things of little importance which might stop at every station. For most of the day after the rush hour the middle platform was shut to the public while fast trains roared through but it was opened up for the fast Portsmouth train and for the 'West of England Express' (as the staff rather grandly termed the semi-fast corridor train for Exeter and Plymouth). These trains called to 'pick up only', and a senior ticket collector in his fine uniform of double-breasted frock and braided peaked cap manned the barrier. Even the stationmaster himself would usually be upon the platform to see these important trains away and to make sure that a large party like ours

Kingston upon Thames Libraries

1. Surbiton station of the LSWR in the year of King Edward's coronation, 1902. The morning rush of black-coated, top-hatted, all-male commuters is over, and horse-drawn cabs wait patiently below the elaborate if rather dim gas-lamps and the massive telegraph poles. The dusty, untarred road will be cut up for tram lines in another four years.

found its ENGAGED carriage safely. That was the slightly ambiguous word always used by the LSWR on a blue printed window label when you had booked six tickets and could have the whole compartment to yourself.

The first premonition of the delights to come was the titter-titter of the signal wires below the platform edge as the signalman in his box, a quarter of a mile away, with a mighty heave of his lever, pulled 'off' the signals. This brought the old-fashioned sema-phore arms down into the lower quadrant position where they seemed always to have a pleasant welcoming look. They were cumber-some, of course, and liable to trouble in heavy snow, but much more interesting than a mere light changing from red to green. Next came the loud ring of the big electric bell on the out-side wall of the waiting-room, indicating that the train had 'entered section' and passed the previous signal-box a mile away; in another minute or so, the great moment was at hand and the front of the engine appeared round the gentle curve of the deep cutting by which Joseph Locke, builder of the line, had sliced through Surbiton Hill seventy years before.

Variety was one of the great charms of railways then, and the locomotive might be one of three or four different types from an old 4-4-0 or a newer 4-4-0 to one of the latest 4-6-0s designed by that fierce old Scot, Dugald Drummond. To be able to identify it correctly at some distance was an essential of boyish pride. As it approached, free-wheeling easily with steam shut off and the vacuum brake being applied, a bluish haze hung over the train and if it had an engine with outside cylinders – like an Adams 4-4-0 – there would be that splendid sight of the up and down rotary motion of the piston rods, like great elbows, the steam loco's glorious *show* of power unequalled by any other machine.

Engine and its separate tender swayed inde-pendently for a second or two as they swept over the points, due probably to the three or four thousand gallons of water sloshing about in the tender, then in came the train. As usual it seemed to miss the platform edge by only an inch or two, wheels rattled heavily and rhythmically over the rail joints and over all was that delectable, unforgettable whiff of coal smoke, steam and warm oil.

That hero, the driver – and he would be a top link man, an aristocrat of the Nine Elms engine sheds – would be leaning slightly out of his cab, in his short blue cotton jacket, with one hand on the vacuum brake to ease the train to a stand nicely at the end of the plat-form. One did not realise then for how many years he had had to slog away, first as an engine cleaner, then fireman, later driver of goods trains, before he reached his present status; or how stiff a 'medical' he had to pass each year. His firemen, too, had to be extremely fit and skilful to be able to keep shovelling coal, accurately placed into the fire-box from the cramped and continually joggling and swaying footplate. The engine itself was im-maculately clean in its light-green paint, richly lined out in black, chocolate and white and with a scarlet buffer beam; the carriages, too, were colourful in their so-called 'salmon' (really biscuit coloured) upper panels and dark brown below.

The ENGAGED compartment was ceremoni-ously unlocked by the stationmaster and the family piled in, each child clutching a small piece of hand luggage while their father took a careful look down along the platform to make sure that the pre-tipped porter was stowing all the luggage in the guard's van. A wave of the green flag and the train moved gently off, jogging over points and rumbling over a big girder bridge across a main road, while the first laboured puffs of the exhaust settled to the soft roar of an engine steaming hard to work up speed.

It was not a corridor train but it did have that splendid period institution of the 'lavatory compartment' – the separate and private accommodation opening direct out of the compartment; in a coach of perhaps seven compartments, four might have their own loos. On many lines this was an intermediate stage before the corridor coach. It was strange in one way for, as Hamilton Ellis has observed, 'A nicely brought up girl or an otherwise tough Victorian matron would take complex precautions to avoid observation when entering the water closet at home – yet in the railway carriage of the time the unmentionable door was there before all the company.' The simple apparatus just 'gave' straight on to the track and when the seat lid was raised you heard an exciting plonkety-plonkety sound from the rail joints below. In fact some very realistic recordings of railway track noises were made in recent days by lowering the microphone down the pan.

At all events, for a family with young children the arrangement was perfect. With a picnic lunch it could be a safe fortress and you were proof against all interruption; best of all (from the parents' point of view) children could be kept under constant surveillance and given a wash and brush up before the journey's end.

If you had the window open – and in summer you wanted the air – tiny particles of unburnt coal seeped in and sooner or later a smut usually went into someone's eye; at the very least a black dust became visible on any pale surface. For all its pleasures steam travel could be dirty, and without vacuum cleaners it was difficult to keep upholstery clean to modern standards. However, there was the added interest that the various sorts of coal used by the

2. Smartly uniformed guard of the LNWR complete with bandolier, company badge, watch and green flag. Typical luggage of the time is the vast trunk in canvas cover on the truck to the right, the ladies' hat-boxes, the leather Gladstone bag, the tin box and the wicker basket probably containing the clothes of the maid travelling with the party. Note also the rings above the doorway for the earlier form of external communication cord.

different companies – and before 1914 there were over a hundred separate companies – produced varying smells in the train. So it was that the South Western, mainly dependent upon Kentish coal, smelt quite different from the Midland with its coal from the north, or from the Great Western with its Welsh coal (the GWR had also a strong odour of gas as it was later than some to adopt electric lighting generally).

The LSWR, except in their very oldest carriages, always provided quite attractive 'Photochrome' colour prints showing 'Holiday Resorts and Places of Interest on this Railway'. Among the views were the Great Globe at Swanage, Stonehenge and Boscastle – all much more fun than the Midland's everlasting list of its hotels. They were all called 'The Midland', which somehow seemed rather feeble, except for Liverpool which had 'The Adelphi' and London where it was styled 'The Midland Grand', which was overdoing it a bit. To be fair, however, the Midland did also have some sepia photographs in their carriages including several of Ulster, reached via Heysham, and, rather surprisingly, of Bath. The London Brighton and South Coast, one felt, was rather low in adjuring its passengers 'in the interests of public health and the prevention of consumption to refrain from the objectionable habit of spitting' – but in those days the warning was well warranted.

Besides the usual notice about the £5 fine for improper pulling of the communication

16

17

3.   LSWR 12.50 Waterloo to Portsmouth express gathering speed as it approaches Vauxhall on the former through line which had no platform. The head-code of the Drummond 'T9' 4–4–0 indicates that the train is to run via Cobham, leaving the main line at Hampton Court Junction and avoiding Woking. Though built in the 1880s, that route at the time of the photo (1909) was still known as the New Line.

cord, the LSWR also had in its compartments an interesting heart-shaped card nailed above the window extolling the merits of the South Western Hotel at Southampton. It ended with the intriguing statement: 'Incoming liners wired from Hurst Castle; porter in red livery meets boats and trains.' Hurst Castle is at a point on the mainland opposite the Needles on the Isle of Wight, so one imagined there was plenty of time for the porter to get into his red livery before the liner had run up Southampton Water and berthed, but how did one man cope with several lots of passengers? And *did* any of them ever decide to go to the hotel rather than to get straight on to London in the waiting boat train?

To revert to that Portsmouth express on an August morning about 1909, as it gathered speed there was that absorbing rhythm of the wheels to enjoy, far more pronounced than it is today when so much of the track is welded and one can scarcely hear the noise of the rail joints. 'Da-da-dun, da-da-dun' they went where there were rails of 45-foot length, then there might suddenly come the change to 'duddly-duddly-duddly' on the older 30-foot rails, which made you feel you were going much faster. Especially satisfying was the fatter noise which came when the train was running along beside one of those retaining walls in a cutting; it sounded like some giant piece of cloth being flapped at you and it took me a few years of boyhood to realise that this exciting extra noise was due merely to the echo of the rail joints off the hard surface of the wall.

It was a journey to the Isle of Wight and one would stop at Guildford and perhaps the tender of the engine would be topped up with water. That was a fine business, to see the firemen get down on to the platform, haul the arm of the water crane out over the tender and train the hose into the tank. It swelled out as the water poured through. Directly the tender was full, the water was turned off by the wheel at the base of the crane and as the hose-pipe was swung clear of the tender there was always a fine splosh as the water still remaining in it cascaded down on the platform. Of course one thought of this fine animal – the engine – having a good drink before the long climb up to Haslemere. Guildford could boast two

other railways in those days and there was always the chance of seeing a neat brown LBSCR tank engine from that pretty little single line from Horsham and Cranleigh, or a handsome South Eastern and Chatham loco going off across country to Reading.

The carriage lighting, if it was electric, was obligingly switched on by the guard as the train puffed off past the engine sheds towards the brilliant white cliff of the tip of the Hog's Back and into Guildford Tunnel. If lighting was by gas it was not so easily controlled in the moving train: then you travelled in the dark, which could be an anxiety for parents of mischievous children (or the chaperones of young lovers). Windows were rather clumsy affairs then, set in the lower section of carriage doors, and to close them you had to haul hard on the leather strap which ran over a small wooden roller fitted mid-way up the door

4. Up the long incline of four miles at 1 in 80 to Haslemere this LSWR Drummond 'T9' 4–4–0 is climbing well, safety valves blowing above a full head of steam. The carriages are Victorian built and gas-lit but some compartments have lavatories; there are two separate six-wheel guard's vans. The diamond-shaped disc on the locomotive's head code indicates the main line to Portsmouth via Woking.

frame. The tunnel was full of smoke and windows had to be shut tight if you were not to be covered with smuts. But once through it – and the very short one which followed – the train was running along the pretty meadows beside the River Wey.

After Godalming came the long climb, nearly eight miles of it and over three miles at 1 in 80, through the deep cutting at Witley, then a high embankment with the view towards Hindhead, followed by the long ascent through woodlands. Up there the engine panted, like some great beast, the cha-cha-cha of its exhaust getting louder and slower as the speed dropped down to barely ten miles an hour. The sound of the wheels sank to a mere dun——dun, dun——dun as each bogie passed over the rail joints. The white blast from the engine's chimney shot high over the surrounding trees, turning black whenever the sweating fireman put on more coal.

Then suddenly came the first bridge before Haslemere, just at the summit, and in a matter of yards you felt you were going downhill and the sound of the engine changed completely. After the stop there it was all a glorious tearaway. In no time the train gathered speed on the downhill run to Petersfield. The former slow 'I think-I-can, I-think-I-can' beat of the engine changed to the happy 'Thought-I-could, Thought-I-could' while the wheels went into a rapid-fire da-da-dun, da-da-dun, and the carriage would bucket about excitingly.

The engine gave a screaming whistle as it flashed through each station and the telegraph wires beside the line rose and fell faster and faster. The much more powerful diesel and electric trains of today have 'flattened out' journeys by climbing so much faster that speed never drops down on gradients. In steam days, to keep his scheduled time a driver often had to go really hard on the falling stretch and it gave much more variety and excitement.

That splendid downhill rush would help to carry you up the next incline, into Buriton tunnel and under the South Downs. Then, after another rush down, the line from Brighton and Chichester of the LBSCR was joined at Havant and soon one rumbled to a stand in Portsmouth Harbour station with oily green seawater to be seen below the planks of the platform.

Always there were plenty of porters about in those days and very quickly that vast collection of luggage would be removed from the guard's van, piled on a trolley and trundled to the end of the platform and the buffer stops where one passed the quietly simmering engine with its crew probably enjoying a swig from their tea cans. Next the luggage was packed into a square, cage-like truck on swivel wheels which was just above the jetty. The whole contraption, with all one's holiday necessities, was then clawed up by a noisy little steam crane which swung it neatly over and down on to the fore-deck of the steamer waiting below. Passengers walked down a convenient ramp to the floating jetty.

The vessel in question was the *Duchess of Kent*, which at the time referred to Queen Victoria's mother – King Edward's grandmother. The ship was a spick-and-span paddle-steamer, one of scores in service around the coasts of Britain, especially on the Clyde, but now obsolete for commercial use. She had a black hull, buff funnel with black top, snow-white superstructure and her name at the bows and scroll work over the paddle-boxes were picked out in gold. She was the joint property of the LSWR and the LBSCR so may legitimately have a place in a book about trains. It was always good to walk up her narrow ribbed gangway, mainly of wood with canvas sides, and then to feel the deck under

5. Ryde Pier and Esplanade station, Isle of Wight Railway, just before the line descends steeply into the tunnel to St John's to avoid spoiling the amenities of the handsome seaside front. This section of line, like the paddle steamers, was jointly owned by the LSWR and LBSCR.

one's feet, smell the sea and have a look around Portsmouth Harbour. There the old *Victory* was still afloat, little naval steam pinnaces with their polished brass funnels fussed to and fro, and if you were lucky you might catch sight of the wonderful new *Dreadnought*, or at least a cruiser or two.

The attractive feature of a paddle-steamer – for boys at least – was that part of the engine room which passengers could view. Because the driving shafts to the two paddles were well above water level (unlike those of a screw-propelled ship) the engines were placed somewhat higher and partly at the level of the main-deck. From behind stout metal fencing passengers could watch the great, gleaming steel cranks at work. One could take up a position in that sweet aroma of warm oil and steam – with a touch of salt this time! – before the ship sailed, then hear the sharp tang-tang from the bridge and see the engine-room telegraph, that great brass indicator, move first to 'Stand By', then to 'Slow Astern'. Next came that 'majestic surge and heave' – as Sir Peter Allen has termed it – the special characteristic of the paddle-steamer as her engines came to life. Thus could be savoured the full dignity of the classic reciprocating marine engine, its polished steel fists punching round and round, working those paddles which drove the ship and left in its wake all that beautiful, creamy foam.

The *Duchess of Kent* had to go astern at first from the jetty in order to execute a Y-turn to get out of the Harbour because a paddle-boat could not turn very sharply. The change to 'Full Ahead' involved more tang-tangs on the engine-room telegraph, more surges and sighs until the engines settled to the steady, deep whoom-whaar, whoom-whaar of their top speed. Like steam locomotives but totally unlike turbines or diesels, the engines of those old paddlers gave a wonderful impression of power applied and work being done.

As the ship approached Ryde Pier Head, after about thirty minutes' progress across Spithead, the high-pitched whistle of a little Isle of Wight Railways engine squealed across the water; it sound remarkably like the feminine shriek of a French engine – wonderfully penetrating but not quite right for anything as serious as a steam locomotive.

One of the charms of the Island has always been that in much of its buildings, equipment and general atmosphere it remains about fifty years behind the mainland; certainly this has always applied to its railways. The whole 'Wight' measures no more than twenty-three by thirteen miles, yet in Edwardian times it had three separate railways, which made it a delightful working museum for the enthusiast. At Ryde Pier Head station there would be two trains waiting, one of the Isle of Wight Railway serving the more populous eastern end, including Ventnor (with its quite heavy 'invalid' traffic all the year); the other of the I.O.W. Central Railway. First one's luggage was swung off the boat and on to the pier – still in the same truck – by another steam crane. Then more porters trundled it over to the train and stowed it in the guard's van. With all the careful labelling one could usually rely upon the guard to put it out eventually at the right station. The wise traveller in charge of a family party would probably go to the van to make sure that all his 'pieces' came out but it was a virtual certainty that they would arrive safely and without the owner having to touch any of it himself since it left his home. An alternative was the Luggage in Advance system by which a railway van would collect it from your home two or three days before you travelled and it should then be waiting for you on arrival at your hotel or lodgings. It was good but cost more and still necessitated

6.   IOWR 2–4–0 tank engine, 'Bonchurch', setting out from Ryde St John's for its run to Ventnor. The little engine was quite handsome in its crimson lake livery; the somewhat primitive four-wheel coaches were built of teak and were oil-lit.

Real Photographs

your taking overnight things with you.

The I.O.W. Railway train serving Brading Junction, Sandown and Ventnor would be drawn by one of the little 2–4–0 tank locomotives built by Beyer, Peacock in 1864. They lasted for over sixty years but the whole 'main line' was no more than twelve miles. Such an engine in 1909 would be immaculately clean in her dark-red livery with bright brass fittings and nameplate as she stood simmering with her Westinghouse brake pump going softly 'paah-paah' as it maintained brake pressure. Behind this rather pretty little engine would be the train of brown teak carriages, all about forty years old, which had been released from Underground service when the Metropolitan Inner Circle line had been electrified a few years before. Lit by oil lamps, they had low divisions between the compartments which did not extend up to the roof and so were rather popular with nervous passengers. The doors had curved tops to them which presented a curiously Victorian appearance, a feature which lingered in other Metropolitan carriages for many years. The most extraordinary thing was that each of these coaches was mounted on eight wheels that were fixed – not on bogie trucks – so that there was apt to be some screeching of wheels on the curves and altogether they rode rather roughly, especially as the Island track at the time was lightweight rail of short length, so that the rhythm of those coaches was mostly 'bump-bump bump-bump'.

Ryde Pier was a wonder in its own right: nearly half a mile long and built of cast iron, which amplified the sound of the train into a roar which could be heard far away, even though there was a strict speed limit. There was a signal-box and some signals on it and you felt surrounded by sea on all sides, but it has stood firm for over a century and solves the problem of the very low tides at that point on the coast. At the end of it, after passing Ryde Esplanade station, the train plunged down at once into a shallow tunnel, to avoid spoiling the beauties of the Ryde front. Beyond the next station, St John's, which was the headquarters of the line, the little engine puffed vigorously, if not very fast, uphill along a single line through pretty woods where wild flowers grew so close as almost to touch the train. So to the important-sounding Brading Junction, a station with at least a passing loop where the Bembridge branch line came in and, if that were your destination, another change was needed. The Bembridge train was an enchanting curiosity with its two four-wheel carriages, acquired from the North London Railway, in one of which was a first-class saloon with separate armchairs in the middle of it. It also ran sometimes a remarkable little coach with open gangways at the end of which enterprising boys might travel, fancying themselves to be crossing the prairies on an early American train.

Such could be the variety of one kind of Edwardian journey, on which there might be as many as eight loadings and unloadings of luggage before it was finally entrusted to another outside porter and his horse and cart for conveyance to the family's 'furnished apartments'.

A journey to the north took one across London and into the territory of another railway. That meant travelling on the despised local train up to Waterloo, in suburban carriages with rather hard seats and drawn by a mere tank engine, probably running backwards, bunker first. That never seemed right, but it was efficient for short runs to have an engine which did not have to be turned at each end of the journey. Actually the porthole style of windows

7. IOWR Brading Junction where one changed out of the Ventnor train for the Bembridge branch line train which is seen to the left of the photo. It is already signalled for departure, the Ventnor train having already left from the other side of the island platform. Now, on the right, the Ryde train is about to leave running bunker first.

at the rear end of a tank engine overlooking the short bunker gave the driver a better view, clear of smoke, than he had when the engine was running forwards. Such a train pottered along, stopping at every station and spending about five minutes at the last one, Vauxhall, where tickets were taken by collectors on the platform who went down the train opening every compartment door. This procedure, apparently so wasteful of time and labour, was necessary for at least a number of trains because many of the arrival platforms at Waterloo — as at other terminals — were entirely without barriers of any kind.

Nearly seventy years ago some motor taxis of very curious shape were to be had but horse-drawn cabs predominated and the smell of arrival platforms often bore witness to the presence of many standing horses, including the not unpleasant scent of their nosebags. A family would usually take a 'four-wheeler' – not a hansom cab – and readers of *Black Beauty* would be in little doubt of the weary lot of the London cab horse as it plodded up the long slope to the old Waterloo Bridge with perhaps four passengers and their luggage.

If the journey was to be on the glamorous Midland Railway the objective would be St Pancras Station and the arrival at that most imposing Gothic structure was an event in itself. Half like a cathedral, it was totally different from the untidy jumble and laby-rinth of Waterloo, then in the throes of re-building. It was the Midland Grand Hotel which caught the attention first and it actually had rubber slabs laid on part of its nearby roadway to dull the sound of horses' hooves for the guests in bedrooms above. An arriving cab would draw up at the *porte-cochère* on the west side, where there were always obliging porters to take the luggage, label it and put it in the guard's van. Then one entered the tasteful booking hall with its linen-fold oak panelling and beyond that was the first glimpse of what were surely the most beautiful trains in all England. Those of some other lines might then be a little faster but for comfort and cleanliness you could not beat the Midland. 'Midland for Comfort' was the sole message on one of their main advertisements – printed actually on the background of their wonderfully rich crimson lake – and they lived up to the slogan. All the passenger trains were painted in this splendid colour (known officially as 'Derby Red'), including the engines, and it was an altogether warmer shade than the dull maroon into which it declined under the fierce economy drives of the London Midland and Scottish management after 1923. Except for the few suburban trains, all the carriages had the handsome clerestory roof which made them look higher than those of many other lines and they were all kept miraculously clean, despite the number of tunnels they had to pass through.

Above the trains there stretched the tremendous arched roof of the station which covered all the platforms in one great span. Its shape acted as a remarkable sounding board so that the blast of a Midland engine starting away always sounded twice as powerful as most others, although the MR was renowned for its 'small engine' policy. For its passenger trains it employed nothing larger than 4–4–0s; it never possessed a 4–6–0 and its heavier expresses were usually double-headed. Such prodigal use of skilled labour was much less serious in days when the top

link drivers probably earned less than £3 a week for at least a ten-hour day.

Travelling in a family party, you might reasonably hope that your father, having settled the females into their compartment, would agree to 'go up and see the engine' – in steam days this was the proper course for any male. Frequently a small gathering would be found at the front of the train, watching for the rear end of the tender to appear as the engine backed down from the sheds at Kentish Town. Even before the loco itself was plainly visible the expert should be able to identify its type from the size and shape of the tender. As it edged slowly towards the front coach of the train the fireman probably dropped off the footplate and trotted ahead on the platform, ready to jump down on the track. Then he had to heave up the weighty coupling of the tender, drop it on to the hook of the leading coach, tighten up the screw section of the coupling and connect the vacuum-brake and steam-heating pipes; that done, he had to re-arrange the lamps on the front of the engine to provide the correct head-code for a 'fast passenger' train. It was all a routine job but called for precise know-how as one false move might risk serious accident or injury. After an admiring look at the driver and his engine, now blowing off under its full head of steam, one would be wise to rejoin the rest of the party in the safe haven of the compartment.

A journey in the supremely satisfactory, and in those days comparatively rare, corridor coach meant that you might stand in the corridor on your own – if you behaved – and have a perfect view of everything you passed on one side of the train. This always included overtaking some of the enormously long coal trains returning empty to the mines of Derbyshire or Nottinghamshire; the express would overhaul them pretty quickly but one had time to

25

count the number of trucks.

Another delight of the corridor train was that it gave you the opportunity to risk sprawling out for a few minutes in a first-class compartment if you found one empty; also you could inspect the lavatory at the end of the passage without the whole family knowing. Midland loos were especially interesting, and were in advance of others because, as you lifted the top lid, the pan automatically filled with water to a depth of three or four inches, which made it seem far more hygienic than those of other lines. A notice on the wall stating that in frosty weather water should be used from the can provided was an interesting reminder that the MR trains to Scotland regularly climbed up to eleven hundred feet above sea level on the exposed moorland section of the line between Settle and Carlisle.

Leaving St Pancras and passing those great gasometers, one was immediately aware of the exceptionally smooth riding qualities of the rolling stock: it just purred along, even half a century before welded track was to become general for main lines. The one disappointment was that, unlike the lines out of Waterloo, there were so many tunnels, culminating in the great Belsize tunnel running for over a mile under Hampstead. But after that the train burst out into sunshine precisely in the words of John Betjeman:

> Rumbling under blackened girders, Midland
>   bound for Cricklewood
> Puffed its sulphur to the sunset where that
>   land of laundries stood.

The Midland's smoke *did* smell sulphurous and there used to be, it seemed, innumerable 'steam laundries' at Cricklewood, but after that there came the grand watery expanse of the lake known as the Welsh Harp, and the flying field then at Hendon where, with luck,

a primitive aeroplane might be seen.

Hertfordshire and Bedfordshire did not offer the most exciting of scenery – nothing to what the MR had in Derbyshire or across the Pennines – but their stations had a charm of their own, with elegant gabled glass platform canopies and often rather pretty Victorian Gothic buildings. Remembered too are the curious open-air cast-iron urinals, set in the middle of their platforms, almost à la Clochemerle, save that the MR variety were more decent and offered total concealment from all but a balloonist! It was a neat and well kept line, having the longest stretch of four-track route in the country, seventy-six miles of it to North Glendon, just beyond Kettering, to enable its many goods trains to be segregated from the passenger expresses. Like other main lines it had its full quota of the then famous advertisements for Hall's distemper (flat wooden figures of two enormous men bearing a ladder between them, each carrying a bucket and brush) and the other celebrated one of the age, a great hoarding for Carter's Little Liver Pills and above it 'London 72 miles' – or whatever the distance might be. At the end of a holiday one was always sad to see the mileage dropping steadily as one neared St Pancras.

With characteristic sharp blast the MR 4–4–0 engine went pounding along up the gradual climb through Elstree and Harpenden, followed by a spanking run down towards Luton and later another fine dash down from Harlington to Bedford. There was also the thrill of picking up water at speed from the water-troughs. Then you had to keep windows closed because the front of the train could be covered in spray and on the glass there was a curious effect as if it was raining upwards.

After seventy miles of smart running Kettering was reached and if, as in our case, the

Photomatic

8. Summer scene of 1908. The skirts of the
light-coloured dresses of the ladies sweep the
platform, and the dark-suited gentleman wears a stiff
linen collar with his straw boater. A SE&CR Stirling
4–4–0 on a Redhill to Reading train, surrounded by a
brake haze, slows to a stop at Reigate. In the
background to the right can just be seen a massive
cast-iron slot machine ready to dispense one of three
different kinds of sweets at the drop of a penny.

27

destination was Market Harborough you had to leave the express to continue its way to Leicester and Derby. An equally spotless local train, non-corridor but also with clerestory roof, took you on and this would be hauled by an ancient and Victorian-looking but rather endearing Kirtely 2–4–0 engine then nearly fifty years old. She was a great contrast to the fine Deeley Compound 4–4–0 of the express. These latter, built in 1905, were some of the most attractive-looking of all Edwardian engines, and the famous No. 1000, restored to the full glory of her original MR livery, is still to be seen in the magnificent display of preserved locomotives at the York Railway Museum.

9 (below). Midland in full splendour: an up Bradford express near Elstree, hauled by a Johnson three-cylinder 4–4–0 compound, in the famous 'Derby Red' with clerestory carriages to match, except for the front one which is a through coach from the L&YR. The engine is, of course, immaculate with even the steel hinges of the smokebox door brightly polished. The flat plates below the engine buffers were to prevent water from pouring over the leading bogies when passing over water troughs with a pilot engine in front which was also picking up water.

10 (right). Midland first class, the acme of Edwardian travel luxury, if a trifle florid. Note the elaborate lincrusta ceiling decoration, the brass fittings for the green baize gas light cover, the elaborate brackets supporting the racks, the inlaid and carved panelling of door and window frames, the blue-buttoned cushions – reversible with leather on the reverse side – and the adjustable foot rest.

29

National Railway Museum

11.   Midland posters left no doubt of its claim to comfort and the remarkably wide span of its through carriage workings, quite literally to all four corners of the kingdom.

2
Steam Locomotives

In Edwardian England steam was the undisputed motive power for all railways except the Underground and certain suburban lines. While the tramcar had begun to cut into traffic on the latter, up to 1910 the steam locomotive was king. One of man's most beneficent inventions, seemingly possessed of a life of its own, it earned great affection from its users. Most engines looked good-tempered and all, seemingly, had an interesting expression about them – it derived from their funnels. The GWR with their shining copper rims had a smiling swagger; the Midland had a hurried, slightly breathless look; the Drummond T9s of the LSWR a serious almost forbidding aspect (like a lady with the very high necked dress of the period) though their successors, the L 12s with the shorter funnels had an altogether more genial look. Again, the LNWR presented a solid no-nonsense aspect as if to say 'we are the Premier Line of England' – dull, perhaps, but solid and reliable.

Even standing still at a station a steam engine was never dead or inanimate so long as it was 'in steam' with its fire alight. It would burble and hum gently to itself even if it were not actually blowing off from the safety valves. Without warning it might squirt out little piddles of boiling water and drop a few red-hot cinders. Track at the point in a station where engines usually stopped was likely to be blackened and oil-sodden. One fitted with the Westinghouse brake always gave a thoughtful 'pah–pah' upon its pump at intervals even when still, and when it first stopped there would be a frenzied pah–pahing for a time while the brake pressure was restored.

With a touch on the injector or the blower the crew might at once change its tune as more cold water was drawn into the boiler or extra draught applied to the fire. When the moment came for an engine to start a heavy train, you could never be quite certain whether it would move off smoothly with a steady measured puff – 'chah – chah – chah' – or whether, on a greasy rail, there might be a thunderous cha–ah–ah–ah–ah as the coupled wheels slipped badly and the engine seemed to stumble like a great cart-horse. Much depended upon the driver's skill with the regulator and his ability to close it momentarily at the beginning of the slip: it was of absorbing interest for the train watcher.

Though much of railway engine working was a dirty job with its perpetual black coal dust and oil it was redeemed by the clouds of snow-white exhaust smoke, its unfailing trade mark, which gave it unforgettable beauty. Even when that was temporarily blackened at the moment of firing there was still something majestic about it. On a frosty morning great puffs of white vapour would hang in the air after the engine had passed and then, from the end of the last coach, would come that 'rabbit's tail' of steam from the carriage heating-pipe.

The iron work-horse of the era for main-line passenger trains was the 4–4–0 type with two inside cylinders. To this was added on many lines the Atlantic type with 4–4–2 wheel arrangement. On the Great Western Railway the first 4–6–0 appeared in 1903, to be followed by the period's one and only 4–6–2 Pacific, the famous 'Great Bear', in 1908. 'Single Drivers' of the 4–2–2 type were readily to be seen on Midland, GWR, GNR and GCR, while smaller 2–4–0 and 0–4–2 engines as well as countless 0–6–0 goods and tank engines abounded. Here, then, were seven different wheel arrangements alone and with sixteen main companies and many lesser and independent concerns, all with their different liveries, it can be realised what variety awaited the enthusiast and how much richer was the railway scene even than that of the Big Four groups between the wars.

While green was the most popular colour for engines, there were many shades from the light grass-green of the London and South Western and apple green of the Great Northern to the dark, so-called Swindon green of the Great Western. The lordly London and North Western, the self-styled 'Premier Line', was content with black for its engines, in marked contrast to its rival the Midland, whose passenger engines were all finished in its unique crimson lake. But what gave the locomotives of the period such distinction was the smart lining out of their livery, and frequently the polished brass fittings on the boiler. Instead of the all-over black so familiar at the end of steam on British Railways, one could be sure to identify at once the individual lines such as the rich dark blue of the Great Eastern with its most striking feature of scarlet connecting-rods to the coupled wheels.

Each separate line frequently displayed its coat of arms on some part of the engine, often a heraldic device which included some of the arms of the cities served by the line with, in the case of the Great Western, an improving Latin tag, 'Virtute et Industria'. Added to these would be the initials of the railway, usually on the tender side, emblazoned in a heavily shaded gilt lettering. This could appear rather bloated to the typographer of today but it presented a fine air of rich confidence, as may be seen from the full-blown splendour of the word 'MIDLAND' as it appears on some exhibits at York Museum.

That most Edwardian engines appeared normally so beautifully clean was the more remarkable when one considers how dirty was the atmosphere of large towns when the open coal fire was the universal English method of domestic heating, while, of course, the conditions of steam railway working were a guarantee that the trains themselves passed continually through fine coal dust spread by every passing engine. The answer lay in the vast pool of low-paid labour then available to all railway companies.

So it was that at the end of its day's duty, whether it had done 200 miles of express work on the main line or twelve hours' shuttling to and from an outer suburban point and a Lon-

12. LNWR Precursor 4–4–0 blasting its way up the famous 1 in 77 Camden bank. From a cold start at Euston it was a test for any engine and this photo is striking evidence of the amount of soot deposited on houses near the line in the days of steam.

13 (above). The handsome small-wheeled Caledonian 4–6–0 designed by J. F. McIntosh, resplendent in its famous blue livery outside the St Rollox sheds, Glasgow. The cleanliness of every detail is clearly visible. The Westinghouse brake pump in front of the cab is a reminder that in steam days all stock working through from England to Scotland had to be 'dual fitted' with both vacuum and Westinghouse brakes to be usable with the different systems operating each side of the border.

14 (left). GER of Victorian vintage but a 2–4–0 locomotive much used on local trains early in the century. Note the four-wheeled tender and the unusual head code, characteristic of that line; the two leading coaches are six-wheelers.

don terminus, an engine returned to the sheds to be set upon by a team of youngsters – in the Great War it was often to be women – who thoroughly cleaned out its fire, raked away the ash, then systematically cleaned the mud and dust mixed with oil which caked the wheels and much of the rest of the engine. On many lines the paintwork would be finished off, after each cleaning, with a fine layer of clean grease which would be worked into a neat pattern and fairly shone in the sunshine. The brilliant reflection of the light from the boilers of engines in old train photographs leaves no doubt as to their spotless condition.

LCGB (Ken Nunn Collection)

Much more than the fear of dismissal if work was not done to the satisfaction of shed-masters – or of the driver who took over the engine for duty on the following day – there was undoubted pride in the job and loyalty to the Line. An immaculately clean loco of the LNWR might be only black, but it could seem as bright as a blackberry in the sunshine and picked out with neat red and white lining. The plain scarlet buffer beam, too, without initial or number, looked very fine, especially when it was clean. The splendour of the general 'turn-out' of several of the independent companies must have done much for their goodwill in the public eye, whether it was the polished copper caps to the chimney tops of GWR engines or the lovely blue of the Caledonian and the Great Eastern. There was also the interesting warm brown shade of the North British and latterly of the London Brighton and South Coast, again with highly decorative lining-out. One of the latter's Atlantics at the head of the spotless rake of cream and umber Pullman cars of the once-termed 'Southern Belle' could be a proud sight. The fact that its whole run was but 50½ miles in the hour on a comparatively easy road is beside the point. It provided a standard of Edwardian service and elegance unique in England at the time. (Even the demise of its electrified version over sixty years later was the subject of sad complaints to *The Times* from distinguished people.)

Beneath the attractive appearance of the locomotives from 1901 onwards there came swift advance in power to meet the growing weight of passenger expresses with the introduction of corridor stock and dining-cars. Where, for example, on the LNWR the first corridor Scotch Expresses in the 1890s had been hauled by two of Mr Webb's tiny engines, probably a 'Jumbo' 2–4–0 and one of the rather unreliable Compounds, and on both Midland and GNR the single-drivers of Samuel Johnson and Patrick Stirling had often sufficed, sometimes with the addition of a pilot engine, the 4–4–0 type became dominant with the turn of the century.

While some 4–4–0s were referred to as 'the latest giant' in the *Railway Magazine*, they were all quite small engines by comparison with those seen in the last days of steam. Yet their performance could be brilliant. 'The City of Truro', the GWR 4–4–0 built by William Dean in 1903, achieved its immortal 100 mph in 1904 – downhill at Wellington in Somerset and with a light load – and a sister engine, 'City of Bath', ran with a portion of 'The Cornishman' the 233 miles from Plymouth, via Bristol, to Paddington at an average speed of just over 60 mph. Seen today in the GWR Museum at Swindon, what strikes one is the very modest size of the 'Truro' and, incidentally, the skimpy protection of its cab. At the same time the layman looks aghast at the immense length of the blade of the shovel, much more than double that of the ordinary kind. Therein of course lay the secret of much of the remarkable performance of those small engines – hard driving made possible only by hard firing. On their heavier duties, like many of the unfortunate horses of the day, they were flogged along as one seldom saw in the later years of steam.

Though the GWR rightly holds its honoured place in the history of Edwardian steam, other 4–4–0s also did magnificent work; those of Dugald Drummond on the LSWR, though introduced in 1899 (and derived from similar locomotives he produced earlier for the NBR and the Caledonian), were famous for their sparkling runs on the switchback of the Salisbury to Exeter line, where speeds up to 85 mph were normal on the best trains. His

T9 class well deserved their nickname of 'Greyhounds'. So, too, on the Midland the 4–4–0 Compounds, first of Samuel Johnson, and later as modified by R. M. Deeley, achieved prodigious feats of climbing and of high-speed running on the level, while the smaller Simple two-cylinder engines of the same wheel arrangement maintained much of the long-distance passenger traffic on that line.

On the LNWR the 4–4–0 came most emphatically into its own in the first decade of the century. The autocratic Francis Webb, who had built countless locos both simple and compound of the 2–4–0 type, had advanced to the 4–4–0 at the turn of the century in his Alfred the Great class of sluggish and unsatisfactory four-cylinder Compounds. It was, however, his successor, George Whale, who gave to that line its enormously effective Precursor 4–4–0 a Simple two-cylinder design which proved immediately reliable and of which over a hundred were built by 1906. The harder they were driven, naturally the fiercer the draught on their fires, and the faster was steam raised so long as a willing fireman piled coal into the fire-box. The London to Liverpool (Lime Street) non-stop run was one of their hardest 'turns' and the late W. A. Tuplin has described the footplate work needed on a Precursor to keep time with a heavy corridor train with two dining-cars. It meant hard pounding with full regulator nearly all the way, and no let-up for the fireman until the last few miles; even the carriage heating turned off at one stage to save steam and scarcely a wheelbarrowful of coal was left in the tender at the end of the run! It was not uncommon to see such engines thunder through a station, when driven hard, with the steel front of the smoke-box glowing red, while at night a shower of sparks flew from the chimney. It made a memorable sight and was more evidence of steam power and of work being done – not perhaps in the most efficient manner, but in those days good steam coal was cheap and the labour plentiful.

For the passenger to travel behind an engine so hard-worked the noise of its exhaust – the puffing – could be a special interest in itself as it varied between the different railways. The LNWR was famed for the sheer loudness of its engines: this may have been partly because, from its London terminus, Euston, all journeys began up the steep incline of Camden bank. In preparation for this start from rest with a technically 'cold' engine, maximum boiler pressure was essential so the fire was normally built up to the point where the safety valves were blowing off with a noisy roar. The longer, narrower locomotive chimneys, or funnels, of those days emitted a much sharper blast and, up between the high retaining brick walls of the Camden bank, a heavily loaded Precursor fairly shouted its way with a peculiarly sharp chah–chah–chah. Passengers who did not keep the windows closed could be sure of a generous hail of smuts into the compartment. With the Precursors' success the LNWR was encouraged to embark upon its first 4–6–0, the inside cylinder Experiment class. This was, in effect, an enlargement of the Precursor but with smaller coupled wheels.

The Midland 4–4–0s were never worked so hard as those of their rival and the slightly different shape of their funnels produced a softer but bustling horh–horh–horh as they

15. Redhill Junction SE&CR looking south in 1909. A Stirling 4–4–0, with its rounded cab roof, on the train leaving the platform, and an 0–6–0 on the goods train to the right. The two through tracks towards the left are for the use of expresses. Typical of the period is the massive signal gantry in the distance controlling the junction points.

hotomatic

16. GNR Bradford Exchange station, 1901, with a Stirling 0–4–2 engine with a domeless boiler but huge, brightly polished safety valve. On this immaculately cleaned engine the pattern of the surface grease is plainly visible. The ubiquitous tin enamel advertisement for Epps's Cocoa is to be seen on the stone retaining wall above.

gathered speed from St Pancras. It was different again from King's Cross, where the GNR engines were said to go 'peppering along' – and anyone travelling towards the front of the train could hear just how the engine was working, whether labouring with a heavy train and a gradient or comfortably master of its job and spinning along on the level. Moreover, the knowledgeable traveller could probably distinguish by the sound of the engine to what line it belonged and – if all else failed – by the sound of its whistle (or,

in the case of the Caledonian its hooter).

Among the famous 4–4–0s of Edwardian days were also those designed by H. S. Wainwright of the South Eastern and Chatham for the Continental boat trains between London, Folkestone and Dover. The shortness of the main line on which they worked and the almost complete absence of corridor trains caused them to be rather overlooked by many enthusiasts; in fact these engines were remarkable in two respects. First they were exceptionally brilliant in their colours, the dark green being handsomely set off by the polished copper top of the chimney, the bright brass of the steam dome and safety valves and the burnished steel smoke-box fittings, while lining-out in four different shades was executed more elaborately than that of any other

38

line. They must have impressed many a Continental visitor accustomed to the dull green or black engines of his own country. Far more important, these 'D' and 'E' Class Wainwright locomotives performed very well over an exceptionally difficult route full of steep gradients and sharp curves. To this day barely one third of it, from Tonbridge to Ashford, can be regarded as a true galloping ground such as exists on most other main lines. More than one of the admired engines of other railways regularly making fast runs to the north would have been hard put to it to keep time with a heavily loaded Dover Boat Train of nine bogies in the early 1900s.

The graceful Single Drivers, those engines with only one large driving wheel on each side, were still making their contribution, notably on the Midland, GWR and the GNR, but the Great Central, Caledonian and GER also used them. They nearly all had an unusually smooth and unfussy appearance in action as they were mostly of inside cylinder design and so lacked the vigorous thrashing motion of the connecting rods of an engine with coupled wheels. An outstanding exception

were Patrick Stirling's immortal Singles on the GNR, where outside cylinders drove on to a huge eight-foot wheel, still giving an impression of striding along even at high speed. Though their design dated back to 1870 they were still in use up to 1907, and on the Midland a few Singles remained until after the First World War, mainly as pilots for double-headed trains.

The Atlantic type with its 4–4–2 wheel arrangement was the Big Engine of the mid-Edwardian period for several lines and the three companies comprising the East Coast route, the GNR, the North Eastern and the North British, all depended upon them. The GNR Atlantics designed by H. A. Ivatt were the best known to those living in the south and were depicted upon thousands of picture postcards as hauling 'The Flying Scotsman', which indeed they did with great efficiency for

17. The classic Atlantic type 4–4–2 of the NER with its spacious cab, huge brass safety valve and richly lined-out livery. Though some of the rolling stock could be post-Edwardian the leading vehicle is a narrow non-corridor lavatory carriage, characteristic of the early 1900s.

Real Photographs

some twenty years, as far as York, where Wilson Worsdell's NER engines took over. If the traveller proceeded north of Edinburgh he would be taken forward by an NBR Atlantic designed by W. P. Reid which, on account of the size of boiler and shortness of its funnel, appeared to be the largest and most impressive of all Atlantics: on picture postcards it was almost invariably shown as tearing across the Forth Bridge with the 'Aberdeen Express'. Though very heavy on coal it was originally the most powerful locomotive in Britain and it became a proud claim for a Scots wife of the time to be able to boast that her husband was 'an Atlantic driver'. These engines also did fine work on the sharply curved Waverley route between Carlisle and Edinburgh and remained in service longer than many engines handling express traffic in the early 1900s.

The six-coupled engine – the 0–6–0 – had been in use for many years on goods traffic but with the exception of the NER 'S' class, for passenger service the 4–6–0, the *really* big engine to a keen Edwardian, did not appear until the new century. It was the inspiration of David Jones of the Highland, though owing to his untimely death the engine had to be completed to the final designs of Peter Drummond (brother of Dugald).

In 1903, however, after rigorous experiment, including the purchase and working under close testing of a De Glehn Compound Atlantic from the Nord Railway of France, G. J. Churchward of the GWR brought out the

18. Five pretty little LBSCR locomotives waiting at Brighton station to handle excursion trains. Each appears to be painted in the famous mustard colour known officially as 'Stroudley's improved engine green', and some have the polished copper rim to the chimney. Their haulage capacity was not great but was adequate for the light trains on the easy route to the South coast.

19. NER Atlantic type 'Z Class' 4–4–2 seen below Princes Street Gardens in Edinburgh. These famous engines hauled most of the heavy expresses between York and Edinburgh far into the 1920s. In the foreground is a characteristic Scottish steel lattice bracket signal post, the counter-weights clearly visible at the base.

first of his most famous Saint class 4–6–0s with their two outside cylinders. They represented a tremendous technical advance upon any other British locomotive of their time, and over the next half century much of the best development in steam traction was to stem from Swindon practice as evolved by Churchward and his successors. Much has been written elsewhere of the mechanical details of this famous breed of engines, with their elaborately built tapered boilers giving exceptional steam-raising capacity and a boiler pressure of 225 lb. to the square inch – compared with the then more usual 180 lb. – the long lap valves, and the ingenious front end design to secure the most efficient use of steam.

Outstanding to the traveller who saw the Saints for the first time was the striking, positively un-English effect of the high running-plate curving up from the buffer-beam to expose almost all of the driving wheels, like an American engine. No previous British 4–6–0 had exposed its vital parts in such a fashion and the footplate itself was set much higher than usual so that driver and fireman were perched far above platform level. Instead of being roughly at your level as you passed the engine at Paddington, they looked down upon you! All this became normal some years later but in 1903 it shocked the pundits who regarded the level running-plate and all-over neatness as the hallmark of a well designed locomotive in this country. Added to

41

20. Hard pounding by a LNWR George V superheated 4—4—0 on the 2 pm Scotch Express ex Euston — 'The Corridor' — near Harrow. The ten or more luxuriously fitted twelve-wheeled coaches, with dining car, represented a huge load for such a comparatively small locomotive and it is no wonder that the 'Georges' were worn out after little more than ten years' service.

Ian Allan Collection

these features was the strangeness of that tapered boiler lacking any dome but with a huge brass safety valve in the middle of it, the 'smile' of the incredibly handsome chimney with its polished cap, the crescent-shaped brass-lettered name-plate on the middle splasher – and there was an engine to be proud of! Its six-wheel tender looked disproportionately small but the line had water-troughs so there was no need for the big 'water cart' tenders of some others, and on the side of the tender were the majestic words 'Great Western' in full plus the Company's crest. Churchward's engines were the greatest advance in Edwardian steam and many who travelled behind them experienced an altogether new sense of power; the sharp bark of their exhaust had a fierce note of compulsion about it.

This Saint class and their successors, the four-cylinder Star class, were unrivalled for their immense speed and power, whether handling the non-stop Birmingham two-hour trains or the heavy West of England expresses. It is significant that where they were tried out on two other main lines, in a friendly exchange, the GWR engines far surpassed the performance of the indigenous loco both in speed and economy of fuel.

Characteristic, perhaps, of the times, little

21. Swindon in 1906, showing Churchward's early two-cylinder 4–6–0 with the high running-plate, exposed coupled wheels and high footplate which surprised so many. The mixture of stock, some clerestory and some with elliptical roofs, and the long destination boards are all typical of the period. The signals show the particularly acute angle of the GWR 'off' position and it is interesting to see that all the rails visible are of thirty-foot length.

British Rail

effort was made to lighten the labour or add to the comfort of the engine crews in the greater efficiency of their splendid machines. The Churchward cabs remained skimpy, giving perhaps adequate shelter against rain at 70 mph but none for a vicious cross wind over the Wiltshire Downs, and it was not until the famous Castle class (direct descendants from the Stars) was introduced in 1923 that the GWR publicity department could play up the great innovation of 'tip-up' seats for driver and fireman. The glittering performances of the original Stars as they lifted the 'Cornish Riviera Express' non-stop from Paddington to Plymouth, 226 miles in 240 minutes, were also due to the skill and intense human endeavour of the two men who, standing to the job for well over four hours in all, drove the train through to time on its tight schedule. That 10.30 from Paddington was probably one of the most exacting 'turns' – for the fireman in particular – in the whole country because the toughest section of the down journey came after Exeter when the punishing gradients of the South Devon line called for maximum steam pressure and the fire at its brightest exactly when it was getting 'dirty' with accumulated clinker. However, that train remains an outstanding technical achievement of Edwardian days, just as the sight of its magnificent engine and chocolate and cream coloured coaches pounding round the curve at Teignmouth between the sea and the red Devon cliffs made a railway picture for all time.

The GWR was the only line upon which, before 1910, you could have a good chance of being hauled by a 4-6-0 if you were travelling for any distance, and to have such an engine was a matter for comment to one's friends. On the LSWR they were a rarity and although Dugald Drummond's first attempt, in 1905 with No. 330, was illustrated as the very latest 'giant' in all the railways books – and the height of her boiler and shortness of funnel did indeed make her look enormous – she was a failure. Her designer who had been so successful with his 4-4-0s had not mastered the problems of larger wheel-bearings and the different forms of steam passages and valve gear needed in a big four-cylinder engine. It was 1911 before he succeeded with the so-called 'paddlebox' engine, No. 433 with its broad splashers above the coupled wheels; she and her sisters became favourites for all the photographers of South Western trains. One lapses into the feminine gender at this point, inevitably, on account of the big-breasted appearance of these locomotives due to the great outward sweep of the smoke-box supports which accommodated the upper part of the Walschearts valve gear. Despite their sometimes fickle performance they could run well when carefully fired and always *looked* enormously impressive but in no sense could they be compared for all-round capacity with the Churchward engines.

Another famous 4-6-0, almost of the period though it appeared in 1912, was that of the Great Eastern, the product of James Holden. Though little more than a much enlarged version of his famous Claud Hamilton 4-4-0s of that line, it had the great advantage of superheating. With its rich blue livery lined out in red, the red connecting-rods and brass-capped chimney, it was another fine-looking engine which did good work for over thirty

22. Up West of England express on the fast and pretty Salisbury to Exeter line of the LSWR. The train is hauled by one of Dugald Drummond's less successful four-cylinder 4-6-0's which were not nearly as impressive in performance as in appearance. The four rear coaches were probably from Plymouth, the dining car with its clerestory roof would have been added at Exeter Queen Street (as then designated) and the leading coach appears to be a non-corridor private saloon.

23. The driver's cab of a Midland two-cylinder
4–4–0 shows the normally spartan conditions in
which two skilled men carried through their hard and
concentrated work for sometimes four hours at a
stretch, in the course of a twelve-hour day. The
driver's position was on the right (as with the GWR,
though some lines favoured the left), the
double-handed reverser is beside him, the brake
lever just above it and the steam regulator at top
centre.

years up to the Norfolk coast and on the heavy Harwich boat trains.

While the superheater came into more general use after the reign of King Edward it was to improve greatly the performance of many of the engines we have mentioned. On the LNWR the success of the Precursors led to the famous George V class 4–4–0s, very similar in appearance but with extended smoke-box, many refinements in cylinders and valve gear plus superheating which gave them for their size an astonishing haulage capacity, speed and economy. They became also one of the most popular cheap tin-plate model engines in gauge o (1¼ inches) beloved of countless schoolboys of the time (and the remarkable fact is that they were imported from Germany where the toymakers of Bavaria found it worth their while to study carefully the details of one of our engines and to produce it in quantity solely for a 'foreign' market). The original Georges on the LNWR were so suc-cessful that they were virtually worked to death on their hard duties before and during the First World War and their reign in ex-press passenger work was comparatively short. They stood, however, as a sensational example of the merits of superheating.

Two other types upon which the traveller on shorter journeys was much dependent were the tank engine and the 2–4–0 or 0–4–2 tender engine. The former were of special importance for suburban services, around London, Man-chester or Glasgow. The popular 0–4–4 tank engine was also found on the South Eastern and Chatham or the Midland and was remarkable for its large numbers and extraordinarily wide range of duties. It handled every sort of train from the South Western suburbs into Waterloo, with some help from the older Adams 4–4–2 tanks; it put in some brisk running with quite heavy trains of main-line stock out to Alton and Haslemere in the rush hour, and was to be found on branch-line duties in Dorset and Devon. Those of the SECR and MR tended to be occupied mainly with short-haul shuttle services into and out of their terminus in London. When the work included bringing in empty express stock from the sidings, the tank engine would frequently act also as rear-end 'banker' to give the train a good start on its journey. This practice continued for many years, notably at Waterloo, and long after the power of steam locomotives had greatly increased. It appeared to be the big moment for the small engine to blast its way down the platform, making as much din as possible, in support of its larger colleague at the head of the train. The increase of soot deposit on the glass roof of the terminus was considerable.

The GNR was another user of particularly good-looking and powerful tank engines in the north London suburbs. They were 0–6–2 types with condensing apparatus to prevent their steam exhaust from escaping in the tunnel between King's Cross and Moorgate. The GER, with the most intensive of any London suburban service, depended largely upon an 0–6–0 design of James Holden with very small driving wheels which accelerated quickly for a steam loco on runs with continual stops at short intervals. The trains themselves on that line, with their hard-seated four-wheel coaches and half partitions between the com-partments, were dreary in the extreme, but the number of trains squeezed through the bottleneck of the Liverpool Street approaches morning and evening was a miracle in days before electric traction and signalling, and in this the little tank engines played their essen-tial part. The unfailing advantage of the smal-ler tank engine was its ability to be worked backwards without inconvenience to the driver;

National Railway Museum

24. Unique gathering of LNWR and GWR stock for
special trains at Caernarvon on the occasion of the
Investiture of Edward, Prince of Wales, in 1911.
Carriages vary from good main-line stock and private
saloons to some ancient-looking four-wheelers. On
the right is an LNWR 4–6–0 on a train of early
corridor coaches. The flat-topped wooden signal
posts are characteristic of the LNWR in pre-grouping
days.

it did not have to be turned every time at the terminus. There were also much larger tank engines produced on some lines before 1910 for express passenger work over short distances. These included the 4–4–2 and 4–6–2 types of the LBSCR, 4–4–2s for the North Stafford and the London Tilbury and Southend, also an unusual and very successful 2–4–2 for the Lancashire and Yorkshire. They are mentioned mainly to show again the immense variety of engines at the time.

Finally, one must not overlook a curious branch of loco practice which had a vogue then, the rail motor. It was a specially built carriage of centre-corridor type with guard's van and embodying a very small steam engine at one end. On the GNR, LSWR and L & Y,

25.   Rail Motor of the GSWR showing the diminutive 0–4–0, outside cylinder side-tank loco as designed for that one particular job – and of doubtful use for any other purpose. The photo would appear to have been taken at the works with the engine posed at the wrong end since end windows (to provide a view ahead) are behind the engine, whereas there seems no sign of any driver's compartment at the opposite (right hand) end. The object was, of course, to operate on the 'push-and-pull' system with the engine always remaining at the same end.

for example, the engine was a separate structure, a tiny four-wheeled creature recognisable by its boiler funnel and cab. On the Furness and on the GWR, however, the engine had a vertical boiler and was entirely built into the coach. The passenger thus had the strange experience of seeing smoke emitted from the roof of the carriage and of hearing the scrape of the fireman's shovel, and maybe the sound of escaping steam, from immediately beyond the end partition of the coach. Rail motors could be driven from either end and were useful on branch lines but suffered from the obvious difficulty that any defect of the engine at once put the whole coach out of action. As their driving wheels were very small, when running they sounded rather like a car in bottom gear. They were eventually superseded by the 'push-and-pull' train – the small tank engine working always from the same end of the train but able to be controlled, through a system of wires and pulleys on the roof, by the driver at the other end. Thus it could run back and forth with the same ease as the rail motor, the fireman remaining on the engine at all times.

26. Rail Motor *de luxe* of the LNWR *en fête* at the opening of the branch line from Prestatyn to Dyserth in 1905. Here the little steam engine is mounted 'in-board' at the left-hand end (the chimney for the exhaust steam can be seen poking through the roof), while the moustached driver is visible at the other end. A compartment with driving controls was provided at each end of the vehicle but the fireman, of course, remained in charge of the fire regardless of the direction in which they were travelling. Male finery of the day is much in evidence, including two boys in Eton suits.

National Railway Museum

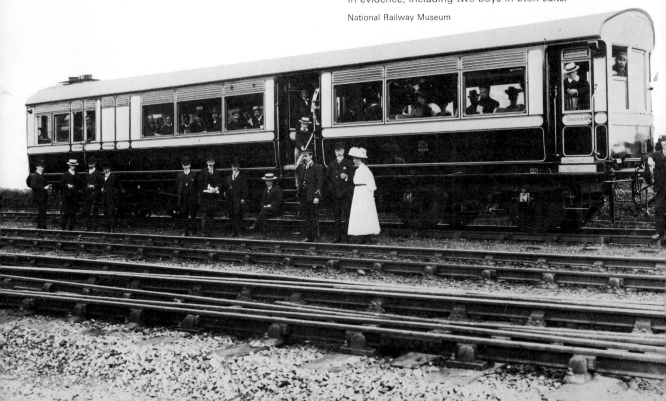

3
Rolling Stock

Edwardian railway carriages, like the engines which drew them, were rich in their variety of colour and design. The period also spanned a great advance in passenger comfort though at its beginning much accommodation was extremely spartan.

Variety at once showed in the number of wheels upon which a passenger coach might be mounted. In 1900 the four-wheel 'bumper' was still common and almost universal on suburban and branch-line trains. Usually lit by gas, such a coach had no means of heating and its riding qualities were far from comfortable. Its rhythm on the short 30-foot lengths of rail was a reverberating 'boom-boom, boom-boom' and the short body was apt to work up an uncomfortable waggle at any speed. The six-wheelers were rather better as each wheel bore less weight than on the four-wheelers and so tended to hit the rail joints less hard. Their 'boom-boom-boom, boom-boom-boom' was more bearable but they too, could oscillate furiously at times, with excessive discomfort to passengers which could lead often to train sickness. Such carriages were quite normal on many long-distance expresses from King's Cross and Liverpool Street at the turn of the century, as well as upon the shorter but still fast runs from Victoria and Charing Cross. For a nervous and less than robust passenger to face such a journey with no chance of the sanctuary of a toilet must have required some fortitude. For other emergencies, there were to be found at the approaches to many terminal stations certain shops which sold curious rubber appliances known as 'secret travelling lavatories' which gentlemen could strap to the leg.

The eight-wheel bogie carriage was in use by the 1880s, even earlier in a few cases, but it was not until about 1900 that it became general upon most main-line trains and during the Edwardian era it grew to be the standard. Many British railway managements had been slow to move on to it, lagging far behind the United States, but this was partly because of the generally higher quality of our permanent way compared with that across the Atlantic. There, the lightness of the rails employed and inferiority of ballast had forced the wider spread of the vehicle weight upon the eight wheels.

It is particularly interesting that as far back as 1876 the Midland had built some magnificent twelve-wheel coaches, with six-wheel bogies, for their new Scottish services – seven third-class compartments and guard's van but no 'loo' – while nearly all other lines used no

27. The polished brass and gleaming blue of the GER 4–4–0 at Brentwood cannot disguise the comfortless rolling stock behind it. All the front coaches of this Clacton train are narrow, low-roofed four-wheelers, probably designated as six-a-side, and must have given a rough ride over the sixty-mile journey. One must hope that the beautifully turned-out locomotive was some compensation for the passengers!

bogie stock whatever. These MR carriages were due in part to the wish to provide greater comfort for a night's journey, with a longer vehicle, at a time when it was difficult to design a four-wheel bogie to bear the weight involved. The twelve-wheel tradition continued for dining-cars on the Midland and later the LMS, up to the 1930s. Such carriages had a rhythm all their own over the rail joints. Instead of the regulation one-two, three-four it seemed to be usually one-two-three-four-five, as more often than not the

adjoining coach had but a four-wheel bogie. It will be readily appreciated that with his alternative chances of four, six, eight or twelve wheels the knowledgeable traveller of the time had his interests catered for on a scale inevitably unknown today!

Roughness of riding was not confined to the six-wheeler. Seventy years ago there were none of the sophisticated methods of track laying and maintenance now standard on British Rail and much less was understood of the science of coach suspension and the exact construction of bogies. Practice varied much between the different lines. The self-styled Premier Line – the LNWR – did have the best track in the world, it was generally conceded, and its trains ran extremely smoothly; on the other hand there was nothing particularly advanced about their under-carriage construction. Again, on the Midland, but also on the little LBSCR, the design of the bogies was so good that the riding quality of the best stock was excellent even though the track, certainly in the case of the latter, was not exceptional.

It was a chancy matter; a great-aunt of mine took her seat in the last coach of a Midland express at St Pancras mainly because it would deposit her nearest to the platform exit at her destination. So great was the swaying about as the train went spanking down through Flitwick to Bedford that the poor old lady found herself quite unable to make contact with the cup of tea which had been ordered from the restaurant car. Being of massive build, she was ill equipped to sit well forward and allow herself to move indepen-

dently of the train, as many learnt to do in days of the rougher ride. To younger travellers some 'bucketing about' was part of the fun of a really good run at sixty miles an hour. Sumptuous as were the interior appointments of many trains then, the quality of the ride could often disturb. Even in the once famous Eagle stock, richly decorated centre-corridor first-class carriages used by the LSWR for their Plymouth to Waterloo American boat trains, complaints were made at the difficulty of keeping dinner plates on the table as the Drummond 4-4-os tore through the night with their record-breaking Boat Specials.

As we have shown earlier, the sounds of railway travel were very much more pronounced long before the advent of air-conditioned coaches and when every compart-

28. Another train of carriages far inferior to the engine; the smart SECR 4–4–0 of 1903 at St Mary Cray is many years younger than its load. The leading van is oil-lit, judging by the big pots in the roof, and the rest of the stock is non-bogie. The high-sided goods truck with its tarpaulin cover, standing in the siding, was a familiar sight.

L&GRP (Courtesy David & Charles)

ment took its main ventilation direct from a window opening. With the different wheel arrangements, from four- to twelve-wheelers, trains had a fascinating language of their own. The chatter of wheels gave to many passengers a comfortable background, soothing some to sleep, for others blotting out interruption and enabling the mind to work unhindered. Many have found a train journey a positive aid to some piece of writing, and its erotic stimulus was well known. Edwardian rolling stock or track might not have produced today's smoothness but it had compensations.

The vehicles of seventy years ago, their bodywork almost entirely of wood, showed strongly their derivation from the stage-coach: the stout timbers, the graceful curves, the neat panelling and so much evidence of good workmanship including the beautiful finish of lining out and varnishing. (The Midland actually applied no less than seventeen coats of paint and varnish for their superb finish.) Unfortunately, on many railways the carriages were not kept as clean as might be, and it was only when one had a vehicle which had recently been through the 'shops' that its full glory could be seen, but much of the fine solid structure could be appreciated even if it were far from immaculate. Upholstery was not always sprung, but stuffed with horsehair and 'buttoned', it was quite comfortable.

The interior of the MR third-class carriages was quite exceptional at the turn of the century and far superior to that of any other line.

29. LNWR first-class non-corridor coach still widely used at the turn of the century for long-distance trains. It had no steam heating but was otherwise very comfortable and a fine example of the solid wooden construction which stood up to accidents better than did the elegant carriages of its rival, the Midland. Though an eight-wheeler, it was not mounted on bogies but depended upon F. W. Webb's curious radial system by which the inner axles were rigid and the two outer axles had two-and-a-half inches' lateral play to enable the vehicle to negotiate curves. Hamilton Ellis relates that such carriages at high speed 'were inclined to give sudden lurches at unexpected moments' and the arrangement was abandoned after Webb's retirement.

National Railway Museum

Their great and shrewd Manager in Victorian times, James Allport, believed in looking after the passengers well; he had been the first to allow third-class travel on the fastest trains and to provide upholstered seats and backs and full-height partitions for that class. In place of the somewhat raw-looking grooved and tongued woodwork of, say, the South Western with its artificial 'graining', the Midland offered for the interior of its main-line stock polished wood panelling in a mahogany finish for the third class and walnut for the firsts. The upholstery of the former was in a splendid rep with a Turkey carpet style of design upon a gold-coloured background and it was always kept clean. Carriage lighting was still by gas, one of the weaknesses of the MR, but they most thoughtfully provided dark shades which could be pulled over the lights for night journeys.

Carriage designers were slow to utilise the full width of the loading gauge, which can permit a width of nine feet, until late into the first decade of the century. Thus the narrower bodies did allow a much wider footboard to be provided and the offence of boarding or alighting from a moving train could be accomplished far more safely. Similarly there was space for a more substantial, not to say ponderous, door handle, many types of which did not just click shut but needed an extra twist of the handle to secure them. One felt that the opening or shutting of railway doors was not to be undertaken lightly and unadvisedly. The sheer thickness of the wood of the door was also in very sharp contrast to the two sheets of pressed steel (tin to the layman) which serve for the modern coach. Finally there was the resounding clunk made by the door as it shut – a splendid noise achieved today only by the more expensive motor cars and very different from the familiar metallic crash even on Inter-City stock.

Inside the compartment one would quickly realise the loss of those extra inches in body width. On most lines five a side in a third class compartment was a decided squash and it was wellnigh impossible for all to sit right back unless some were slim young women (they tend to cross their legs while men more often sit with legs apart). Where a company such as the GER or the GNR built wider carriages for their commuter traffic, they then tried to squeeze up to six a side, which proved even worse. You were in trouble, too, in the early third-class corridor coaches where it was supposed to be four a side; one of them needed to be a child if you were to travel in tolerable comfort. At the other extremity was the luxury of many lines such as the LSWR, which expected only two a side in its first-class corridor compartments and, in a less democratic age, there was the convenient middle course of second class. Here, you were upon a cosy-looking brown and black buttoned upholstery, and seated four a side in a non-corridor compartment with a small arm in the middle and arms in each corner under the window. Doubtless reflecting the South Western's concern for the infinitely fine gradations of the middle class to be found in its great residential territory of West Surrey and Hampshire, 'second' was not abolished until 1918, much later than on most other lines.

Every compartment door was marked for its class, usually in neat capital letters of gold, though the Midland, SE & CR and GER were among those who appeared to doubt the literacy of their travellers, for they used instead bold numerals on the lower panels of the doors. This handsome gold leaf also extended to the initials, and often the crest, of the Company and to the actual number of the coach. On the LSWR each door had also

British R

30. High-quality GWR third-class compartment which, though post-1914, displays the best of Edwardian characteristics: roller blinds for windows, drop window in the door which had to be raised by a leather strap; bold figure **3** to indicate class (in case you could not read), framed photographs above the carefully buttoned upholstery and padded arm-rests for the corner seats.

on the inside, just below its window, the coach number as well as a letter to identify the particular compartment.

Above the door window was a sliding panel for ventilation from the set of louvres built into the top of the door. This refinement dated back to the earliest days of railways and was adopted by nearly all carriage designers despite the amount of expensive handwork involved in making it and the extent to which it collected smuts from the engine. There was, anyhow, the elaborate circular ventilator

(often two) set in the ceiling of every compartment and attached to the so-called 'torpedo' ventilator air-extractor, the device responsible for so many of the knobs seen along the roofs of old carriages.

Associated with ventilation comes heating and in 1901, for comfort in cold weather, except on the best trains, the long-distance traveller usually had to depend upon a thick overcoat, kept on throughout the journey, a rug and the famous 'foot-warmer'. This was a flat metal can, about two feet long, filled with hot water and some sodium acetate crystals. As it cooled a shake induced a chemical action which caused the water to warm up again temporarily. If lucky one obtained this device from a large barrow upon which they were loaded at more important stations and on some commuter trains a 'regular' would choose a compartment which would be known to stop near the barrow. At a terminus, porters trundled the barrow alongside the train supplying foot-warmers free but expecting a tip of at least sixpence. As late as 1906 it was still newsworthy to describe the latest carriages as being steam-heated but by the end of the decade this great boon had been generally adopted.

Other hand-made items of carriages were the luggage racks of the day. On a wooden frame, they were made up basically on the principle of the string bag and were quite inadequate for anything substantial. Though they bore the inscription 'For Light Articles Only' or 'Not To Be used for Heavy or Bulky Luggage' they were frequently, like the engines of the day on the LNWR, overloaded, especially on those lines such as the Midland, the East Coast route and the GWR which had carriages with the clerestory roof. This added

about twelve inches to the height in the centre of the compartment and suitcases could be piled up into the extra space. However, in defence of the design of those 'racks', it must be stressed that the majority of people then expected to travel with a quantity of luggage which there was no question of having with you in the carriage. At the start of the journey there was a careful division made, and precise instructions issued to your porter as to which items were to be 'taken with you in the carriage' and which 'for the van' – the latter all having to bear the Company's label. In many an attic or junk shop one may still find old leather trunks with such printed labels as 'Great Eastern Rly' (very small) followed by 'CROMER' (very large). It was quite a task for the porter having to use a paste-pot and brush for each label and to find a suitable spot on bicycle or pram to affix it – and this for perhaps eight or ten 'pieces' – all with an eye to

31. The once famous 'bird cage' look-out for the guard clearly visible on the leading coach of the SECR Pullman train from Charing Cross to Hastings in 1910. It is passing Hither Green 'C' box.

the departure time of the train and ultimately his tip. The maintenance of a stock of labels for virtually all the Company's stations at every station of any importance would have been another of those laborious – and not inexpensive – jobs which railways undertook for the convenience of their customers.

The make-up of the average passenger train before 1914 indicated very clearly this separation of luggage from passengers. Old photographs frequently show an entire vehicle, the so-called brake van, behind the engine devoted wholly to luggage. Some lines had neat six-wheelers which exactly matched the rest of the stock, others went in for larger bogie vans. For the Continental Boat Expresses there were flat cars for the containers of registered luggage to be swung direct from train to ship. Where trains were made up of sets of four coaches it was usual on many lines for about one quarter of the set to consist of guard's and luggage van, each of the end vehicles being technically a brake composite. That is

to say about one half of its length was for luggage and the guard, the rest for passenger compartments. One suspects that, save for holiday times, much of this space was wasted, but its existence clearly showed that the Edwardian did not expect to carry his own luggage into compartments and to test his strength on heaving it up into the rack. It is curious that England lagged so far behind Continental countries in the provision of larger racks made of metal; they did not become standard here until some fifty years after one saw them regularly in France or Germany.

Those guards' vans had two features which again emphasise the handwork lavished on the wooden bodies. One was the care taken to simulate 'blind' windows on the blank outside walls by means of panelling – the space was all carefully marked out by inset panels of the same size as the windows. It looked very well when it was clean but of course the raised edges of the panels all acted as collectors of dirt and added to the labour of cleaning, long be-

32. Royal train of King Edward VII drawn for part of its journey by L&Y 4–6–0 designed by George Hughes. In the centre of the train are the superb saloons designed for the King and Queen by C. A. Park and built in 1903 by the LNWR at Wolverton. These fine carriages are still to be seen at the York Railway Museum. The general glitter of the occasion is enhanced by the highly polished buffers and coupling rods of the engine and the whitened wheel rims of the train.

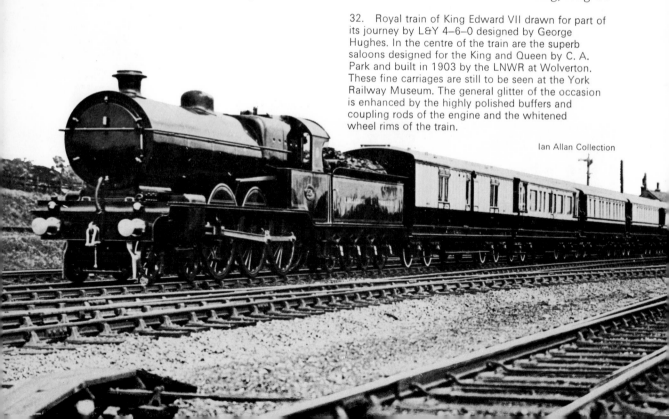

fore the use of automatic carriage washers (unknown before the late 1930s) and when the work was done by men with pails of water and long-handled mops. The second interesting feature was the 'ducket', that section of the van which bulged out beyond the side and, having a little window in it, enabled the guard to squint along the side of the train in motion to see that all was well and to keep an eye out for signals. It resembled a tiny bow window with a seat in it and, as there were always two – one each side of the vehicle – it was a perfect place for any child who had been put 'in charge of the guard' for a journey on his own. For those considered a little young to be quite independent it was a splendid way to travel. The guard of the time appeared always to be a dignified father figure, probably moustached, resplendent in his braided peaked cap, double-breasted uniform with bandolier, leather pouch, whistle chain and flag. His sense of power and control seemed absolute as he stood on the platform at the stops, often some yards ahead of his van, gazing along the length of the train. Then a glance at his watch, checking it maybe with the station clock, a blast on his whistle, a wave of the green flag and always an easy swing on to that comfortably broad footboard as the door of his van moved past him. It appeared always a matter of pride in his case to board the *moving* train which, steam drawn, started away more slowly than today.

A variant to the ducket for the guard's look-out along the train was the South Eastern's unusual form of little glass-house – familiarly known as the 'bird-cage' – which was built on to all their guard's van roofs from an early period. Certainly it is to be seen in photos of their boat trains in the last century and throughout the 1900s and on their four-wheeled suburban stock. Only the rela-

tively low carriage roofs made it possible; such an arrangement could not have worked with carriages built up to the full dimensions of the loading gauge. The guard had to ascend a few steps to get up to his eyrie but he then had an unobstructed view in all directions (it is doubtful, however, whether a 'child in charge' would have been able to share it!).

The advance of the side-corridor carriage was the feature after 1900. The first corridor train appeared in 1892 on the GWR but though it had the flexible vestibule connections between coaches these were used only by the guard, or ticket inspectors, and were kept locked to passengers.

The more general use of the corridor train began in 1893 when the three main lines to Scotland, the LNWR, the Midland and the GNR, all adopted it for their main services across the border. The North Western's afternoon express with the new stock, leaving Euston at 2 p.m. made such an impression upon the staff that it was at once dubbed 'The Corridor', which term railwaymen continued to use for it long after such carriages were standard for any long-distance train. With these particular trains came acceptance of the great principle that third-class passengers should be allowed to use the dining-cars; hitherto their use had been restricted to first class, except on the GER boat trains to Harwich.

It is difficult to imagine what comfort and relief from anxiety the new trains must have given to many travellers. Though one still had reasonable privacy, no unaccompanied lady need feel unduly worried if joined alone by an unknown man; if she disliked the look of him she could change her compartment at any time. A decent hot lunch, moreover, could be had by walking along the corridor, and paying no more than 3s 6d (17½p), instead

59

of having to attempt the awful scramble of the twenty-minute stop for refreshments at York or Swindon. For this modest sum the LNWR was offering, in 1906, no less than 'Soup, Poached Salmon, Roast Sirloin, Roast Chicken and Salad, Asparagus, Diplomat Pudding, Cheese and Dessert', after which Coffee as an extra at 4d seems almost expensive.

Not least there was a lavatory to be found at the end of the corridor in each coach. Usually ignored in accounts of train travel in the past, it is easy to underestimate the anxieties and intense discomfort which must have been caused by the reluctance of railway managements in Britain to make decent provision for human needs. It is true that from the 1880s some lines had provided lavatories for first class and later it was recognised that the thirds should be provided for on the best trains, but the invaluable lavatory carriages

33. Midland goods yard near Birmingham, showing the great variety of different trucks, loose-coupled and with only handbrakes, by which the freight of the country was handled seventy years ago. The very few gas lamps visible remind one of the dangers and difficulties of night work at that time.

already mentioned in our first chapter were rather rare, and it was not until the corridor train that all men, women and children could be saved from possible embarrassment. In North America and in Continental countries the greater distances travelled had forced railways to make reasonable sanitary provision much earlier.

A meal in the earlier dining-cars of some lines had its excitement. One recalls the ceaseless tinkling of the knives and forks on the luncheon tables of an LSWR West of England Express Restaurant Car as it rushed along the level stretch of the Axe valley near Chard, how it shook itself as its bogie hit a rough rail joint on the Axminster curve and how glad one was of the gauze strips at the tops of the open windows as smoke poured from the engine on the ensuing long climb up the Seaton Bank. On the thirty-foot rail lengths of earlier days the chatter of the wheels at speed was a rapid-fire 'duddly-duddly-duddly' and continual vibration which was thrilling for the young but created its problems. The GWR, as notoriously fast runners, had a habit of attaching at Birmingham a restaurant car to the tail end of their up Birkenhead expresses. They then ran exceptionally hard to reach Paddington in two hours and the oscillations imparted to that last coach on the train could be dramatic.

Another variety in the composition of trains was the now unknown slip carriage which, as its name implies, was slipped from the rear of an express to come to rest at a station where the main train did not stop. Many lines used them before 1914 and the GWR continued the practice into the 1930s. 'The Cornish Riviera' was always the heroic example with three separate 'slip' operations: Westbury, where a portion for Weymouth was dropped; Taunton, where a Minehead section was left; and finally two or three coaches for Exeter. Thus the load for the engine was considerably lightened before it had to tackle the hardest part of the journey. Each slip coach was as a complete

34. A well-ventilated van specially designed for 'Fruit and Milk Traffic' for the LNWR. Fitted for the vacuum brake, it could be run at high speed and was sometimes to be seen at the tail of passenger trains. Its exact destination was scrawled in chalk on the small boards fixed to the sliding doors and it bore the standing instruction, 'When empty to Willesden'.

train in itself with first- and third-class compartments, lavatory and guard's van with separate guard. As the express neared the station the guard on the slip coach pulled a lever which disengaged the coupling (and he also sealed off the vacuum-brake and steam-heating pipes); then he applied the brake to stop his coach at the right point on the station platform. If you were travelling in the slip it could be rather exciting to look out of the window and watch for the moment when you parted from the main train – it might be nearly a mile before the station if you were travelling fast – then there was the curious sensation of arriving quite quietly at the platform while the main train was already far on its way. The disadvantage of the operation was that passengers in the slip coach had no corridor connection with the rest of the train, so could not use the dining-car, and, of course, the railway had no means of reversing the procedure. Even the mighty 'Cornish Riviera' itself had to stop at Exeter on its up journey to Paddington to pick up the coaches 'slipped' on the previous day. Still, it was an enterprising way of giving certain towns a faster service, at least in one direction, than they might otherwise have enjoyed.

Associated with the slip idea was the through carriage, which was another labour-intensive but highly convenient arrangement for earlier travellers. Many lines including those to the north provided them but the LSWR probably offered the greatest number on any one train in their morning West of England express, the 11 a.m. from Waterloo. On occasion this could carry coaches at the front for Plymouth, then for Padstow, for Bude, one or two for Ilfracombe, then one each for Sidmouth and Seaton. Each one would bear its separate destination board, white lettering on a red background, and very careful selection of one's

carriage was necessary. Even the rear one for Seaton, which came off first, had its corridor connection with the rest of the train so that it was possible to use the restaurant car so long as you returned to the compartment before your coach was uncoupled. For each of the above destinations the through coach (usually the last) was dropped at the junction on the main line, then shunted on to the branch line train and thus trundled down to the seaside resort without your having to change at all. The whole process went through in reverse for a return journey, the train starting from Plymouth with but four coaches and gradually collecting the rest from each of the aforesaid junctions and normally the dining-car at Exeter. So much coupling up and separation of corridor coaches (with their cumbersome 'bellows' corridor connections between each vehicle and old-fashioned screw couplings) involved again a fantastic amount of hand labour.

Besides guiding the passenger to his proper coach, those destination boards gave railways a chance to advertise themselves rather grandly; many enjoyed displaying huge boards at roof level, just above the windows, bearing such inscriptions as: 'PADDINGTON EXETER PLYMOUTH AND PENZANCE' or 'PLYMOUTH BRISTOL SHREWSBURY VIA SEVERN TUNNEL' to show off the GWR, while the LNWR announced upon the Corridor composite coach (combining first and third class plus guard's van): 'LONDON (EUSTON) LLANDRINDOD WELLS

35. Slip coach of the GWR: a rare view of the guard's compartment showing the special window, facing ahead, which he could lower to enable him to turn off the taps controlling the heating and vacuum brake pipes between his coach and the last one of the main train. The lever below it, when pulled, opened the coupling hook to release the 'slip' which then began to drop behind the train. Ultimately the guard brought his coach to a stop at the station by applying the brake handle to the right (just below the pressure gauge).

& CENTRAL WALES', or again at King's Cross you might see 'KING'S CROSS & ABERDEEN VIA FORTH & TAY BRIDGES'. It could not fail to impress the public and give railwaymen pride in their job even if the value of such boards on carriages could scarcely be quantified to satisfy accountants. One mother, however, never forgot their use on one occasion. She was seeing off her schoolboy son at Paddington and, at the crucial moment of handing him his rail ticket when he was already in the train, between them the ticket somehow slipped down between carriage and platform on to the track. Horrified, she summoned a porter, who went off without a word to the lavatory at the end of the corridor and collected the soap. Then taking down the long carriage destination board from above he rubbed soap over one end, stuck it down to adhere to the ticket visible on the track below and returned it

safely into the hands of the young traveller.

Two other sorts of through carriage should be mentioned briefly. One is that splendid piece of Victoriana, the Family Saloon, which continued some years into the new century before being ousted by the motor car. It was the rich man's form of that lavatory carriage: it was, at its best, a bogie coach with about one half of its area devoted to an open saloon, usually with sofas running lengthways, some separate chairs and a table, then another, smaller compartment for servants, a separate one for the luggage, and a lavatory. A family

36. A convenient through coach working from Deal to Birmingham in 1910. The SECR 0-4-4 tank engine running bunker first, having brought its little train via Addison Road (Olympia), is just joining the LNWR line at Willesden Junction. The SECR brake van with the inevitable 'bird cage' is followed by two LNWR non-corridor composites each, with first and third class and a guard's van in the centre.

LCGB (Ken Nunn Collection)

could travel thus in great comfort and freedom from anxiety, accomplishing such complex journeys as from Dorking on the SE & CR and through or around London and on via the East Coast route to Inverness on the Highland Railway, without change of train. The other carriage worthy of mention was the Invalid Saloon, in which the patient might remain in bed all the way, yet be accompanied by family and servants; it operated upon a similar basis.

For a night journey to Pitlochry in Scotland some eighty years ago my grandfather chartered such a saloon for my grandmother, a martyr to rheumatoid arthritis, and he persuaded the Midland Railway to stop its night express about midnight at his home station of Market Harborough. The stationmaster stayed up to see the party safely into their private carriage but there was consternation when my grandmother realised that the bed was fixed 'facing the engine' and to travel thus was believed to make her sick. To hold the train while the saloon was run out into the yard and on to the turntable was too much even for the MR but the resourceful stationmaster saved the situation by pointing out that the train reversed at Leeds and thereafter she would be travelling 'back to the engine' (as a new one tackled the long climb over the Settle and Carlisle section). In the event all was well but it was a good example of a Company's consideration for its customers.

An appendage to many a passenger train was the horse-box. A little four-wheel van, it was fitted with vacuum or Westinghouse brake so that it could be run with ordinary stock. Within well padded stalls three horses could be comfortably accommodated while their groom (or grooms) had one upholstered seat in a half compartment, oil lighting and no heating, so that relatively they were worse off than the horses! The horse-box was once a familiar sight bobbing about at the tail end of an express, and it must have given a rough ride to many of its occupants – small wonder that more and more of this traffic was lost to the road as the large motor horse-boxes came into use but it was once a valuable part of railway business and sidings at Newmarket and Epsom could be crammed with the little horse-boxes at certain seasons of the year. Another was the flat-truck used for the conveyance of the horse-drawn carriage, or the early motor car, of the well-to-do traveller by train who liked to have his own road vehicle with him on a holiday. Both were useful services provided by railways which added yet further variety to the appearance of Edwardian trains.

Before motor transport had developed seriously the freight business of railways was enormous and any rail traveller was soon aware of it. 'Goods' was the backbone of most railway profits and the archaic looking four-wheeled open goods truck, loose-coupled and with no automatic brakes, was the backbone of that traffic. Dependent only on the brake power of engine and guard's van, slowly but steadily the great goods trains plodded across the length and breadth of England, seldom at more than 30 mph and usually drawn by 0–6–0 tender locomotives, frequently of considerable age. Wherever they stopped the air rang out with that now forgotten ting-tong-ting-tong of buffers clanging together, one after another, as the couplings slackened and each truck slowed down mainly by hitting the one in front. Not until after nationalisation did our railways follow those of other industrial countries and adopt the screw coupling and continuous brake for goods vehicles. Meanwhile our primitive goods trains had an undoubted charm of their own, sorry as one might feel for the unfortunate cattle jammed together in their open-sided trucks and subjected to sudden vicious sideways jerks at the starting and stopping.

A single train might carry seventy or more trucks and as it passed with the unending dun-dun-dun-dun of its evenly spaced wheels one could often see the trucks of at least half a dozen different railways, their large initials plainly marked on the sides, as well as the privately owned trucks of individual firms. Coal often predominated but there could be stone, sand, gravel, ballast, machinery of all kinds under tarpaulin covers. There might be the special vans for fruit and meat and fish, though such perishables normally went by special fast trains which did have continuous brakes. Apart from these through trains were the local goods trains which stopped at every station, uncoupling one or two trucks here, picking up some there. To the interested spectator the engine seemed to enjoy playing about gently in the sidings and constantly producing the sound of clashing couplings and buffers, then standing quietly singing to itself with driver and fireman taking their ease, waiting for the line to be clear for their progress to the next station. Motor transport has killed that class of railway freight but seventy years ago it carried the business of the country.

37. The once universal horse box: the large lower centre panel, when unbolted, let down to form a sloping gangway up which the horse was led (one hoped) into its quite comfortable, well-padded accommodation which could take up to three animals. The groom or grooms travelled in the half compartment to the right whence they could feed and keep an eye on their charges. The 'fitted' van with its vacuum brake could be run on passenger trains.

4

Railway Staff

The railways of Great Britain were run in the first decade of this century by an army of some half-million men upon whose hard labour, skill and devotion to exacting duties the entire system depended. Railway work was seen in the Victorian era as a secure and much-valued form of employment, but its great curse was length of working hours. A well-known story – and a true one – is that of the guard who had been on duty for eighteen hours and was asked to go out again on yet another journey. When he protested he was curtly told by his superintendent: 'You've got twenty-four hours in the day like every other man and they are all ours if we want them.' On another occasion a goods guard, almost asleep on his feet after an excessively long spell, agreed to go out again only when told that he could have a man with him to keep him awake by talking to him.

Although footplate men did not have to endure such intolerable hours, even for them a twelve-hour stint was normal. It is significant that as late as 1906 Driver Robins, whose error of judgement wrecked the LSWR American Boat Express from Plymouth when he took the Salisbury curves at 67 mph, had at the time been continuously on duty for $9\frac{1}{2}$ hours. Had he not been killed outright he would have

had nearly another two hours' driving, at high speed, ahead of him before he would have been due for rest. It remains a miracle that under those working conditions there were not more 'inexplicable' disasters like those at Grantham and Shrewsbury.

These isolated incidents are recalled merely to underline the hard conditions under which railway work was performed in the past and to pay tribute to the indomitable qualities of the men who did it.

The standards of pay, while appearing ludicrous at first sight, were not out of line with the general level of the times, especially when the regularity of railway employment is remembered. Drivers were naturally the most favoured with from 28s to 45s per week (from £1·40 to £2·25); even these rates had tended to fall somewhat in the depression of the 1870s and there was no appreciable increase until the 1914 war. Passenger guards came next with goods guards below them. Further down were signalmen, then shunters, and porters came at the bottom of the scale at between 15s and £1 a week, plus tips. At almost every level, notably of course drivers and signalmen, the responsibilities were considerable and the potential dangers from carelessness enormous. The marvel is that these men, most of them

originally with little formal education, should have grown into so fine a body with much technical expertise and a great tradition of their own.

Draconian as the early working rules appear today, it is understable that the original railway managers considered it essential that their staff should be subject to discipline of military severity and some of the original managers were actually retired army officers. Unhappily the conditions of service were, for many, quite as dangerous – if not more so – than those of the peacetime army. Over twenty-five years up to 1900, no fewer than 12,870 railwaymen were killed on duty, averaging

38. A typical gathering of railway station staff, probably Sandown, IoW, about the turn of the century. The station-master sits between his two lieutenants in the middle of the front row, and the man in mufti to the right is probably the senior signalman. Despite the royal example no beards are visible but the moustache is almost universal. All but three are in uniform and wear the starched collar which required a skilled hand to launder it.

over 500 a year, and in this it seems inevitable that those responsible for the long working hours must have borne much of the blame. Yet with these obvious disadvantages railway service drew intense loyalty and attracted families of men through generations.

68

39. 'At the time of the accident the signalman had been on duty for thirteen consecutive hours' was the phrase from a Parliamentary Report which prompted Felix Moscheles (1833–1917) to paint this picture. Now in the possession of the National Union of Railwaymen, it is mute testimony to the hardship endured by many in railway service over seventy years ago.

A driver waiting on the engine of a local train at Harrogate station in 1950 said, 'My grandfather worked for George Stephenson, my father for the North Eastern, and I've worked for the London and North Eastern' (into which the NER had been absorbed at the Grouping of 1923), then he added 'but my son will not work for British Railways.'

Another man recalled that with his father and two uncles, all driving for the LSWR, his grandmother had had to wash, every week, three pairs of overalls to make sure that her men were properly turned out for the foot-plate. Living in the little railwayman's cottage with no constant hot water, she must have had to do her washing in the copper of a back washhouse, bars of Sunlight Soap flaked by hand, the clothes rubbed hard on a wooden scrubbing board and wrung out finally in a great iron mangle. Detergents and drip-dry garments were fifty years in the future! But no complaints were recorded, just the boyish memory of listening fascinated to the drivers of the family describing their different trips – whether good and easy, or rough with a badly steaming engine. That young man fulfilled his ambition first to fire and then to drive Bournemouth expresses. This leads us beyond our period but is mentioned as proof of the enthusiasm and pride in the job which was at the heart of the most vital part of the steam railways of King Edward's day.

The good engine driver was a craftsman sensitive to his machine besides being a mechanic and also possessing full knowledge of the Rule Book and 'the road' – the stretches of line over which he worked. Besides knowing all his signals, exactly where they were placed and the precise message which each one indicated on a complicated gantry at a large junction, he had to know like the back of his hand every change of gradient, where maxi-mum power was needed, where again the engine might be eased and steam pressure recovered and, not least, the steep down gradients where speed must not get out of hand. This same knowledge of the road also applied to his fireman. Above all the driver's duty was to run his train to time exactly according to the working timetable, stopping where it required and arriving punctually at his destination.

The average passenger did not realise that the engine crew had normally spent an hour preparing the engine before it even left the engine-shed: the driver checked the quality and quantity of coal, the water in the tender and the essential tools, shovel, fire-irons, bucket and oil-cans, followed by a meticulous look over all the oil-boxes and topping them up with oil if needed. The firemen made sure the sand-boxes were filled and working correctly, that the smoke-box door was a good tight fit and that there were couplings at both ends of the engine; then his main task was the gradual building up of the fire – lit earlier – to generate enough steam to send the pressure gauge up to the point where the safety valve would start to blow. Enginemen had only the crude hand naphtha flare to provide light on such inspections and tiny oil lamps to illuminate dials in the cab. Electric lighting was unknown on steam locomotives until the Merchant Navy Pacifics of 1941.

Once they had backed down on to their train, coupled up, tested brakes, arranged the engine head code, received from the guard a note of the number of coaches on it, indicating the weight to be pulled, and eventually started away, much the hardest physical work fell to the fireman. He might have to shift three tons or more of coal on a 200-mile run even with the comparatively small engines of the day and this in exceptionally awkward conditions.

The cabs had less space than those of later engines, and being right at the rear end of the vehicle were subject to the maximum of vibration and swaying at speed. Then the tender on its separate wheelbase had that independent movement of its own. To fill the shovel there and to turn across to the engine side of the footplate, then to shoot the coal faultlessly into the narrow fire-hole, placing it in exactly the right part of the fire – 'filling the holes' – called for consummate skill as well as a powerful pair of wrists and shoulders. Many of the express runs of the time, with the small engines still hauling the heavier trains, put firemen to a more severe test than was the case a generation later. The larger engines were usually not worked so hard as were the 4-4-0s of the 1900s and they called for less skill in the placing of fuel in the fire-box.

On the run the essential of the driver's job was to watch all signals which concerned his train and ideally to work the engine economically while keeping time. The smaller engines had one great advantage: their lower boilers enabled large circular spectacles to be fitted in the front screen of the cabs, thus giving enginemen a much clearer view ahead than

40. The engine sheds at Newhaven, Sussex, showing the shedmaster (and his lady) posed in front of his quietly simmering charges, three LBSCR locomotives. The 0–6–0 goods engine no. 554 is well stacked with coal in her tender and liable to drop some by the line-side, one suspects; the double lamp head-code on the buffer beam was a characteristic of the line.

National Railway Museum

41. LSWR Bournemouth sheds show the
hand-operated steel and wood hoist used to lift the
handsome 'T6' 4–4–0 Adams locomotive which
itself looks superb apart from its lack of the leading
bogies. This and the following illustration are
examples of the primitive workshops from which the
fine engines of the period emerged.

was possible later with the bigger engines. One looked slightly down upon the boiler and there was far less need to get half frozen in cold weather by looking out over the side. By comparison with diesel or electric power everything about the controls of steam was immensely ponderous: the massive lever of the regulator, a strong heave on which was needed to admit steam to the cylinders and to start the engine; the heavy handle of the reverser; the solid brass of the steam-pressure and vacuum-brake gauges; and the thick glass of the water gauge. It was all very much a man's world – no comforts – but built to last out thirty or forty years of hard service, of continual rattle and vibration.

The best crews formed a perfect team: the driver of course was totally in charge but would keep an eye on his fireman, sometimes relieving him with the shovel if the work was exceptionally hard, while the fireman then watched the signals. Some drivers, indeed, made a point always of keeping their hands in on a little firing. A good fireman was always on the look-out for those signals which, on a curve, he could spot earlier than could his mate from the other side of the engine, and naturally it was his pride and duty to ensure that at all stages of the journey he had his fire in such a state that it would enable the boiler to produce the steam pressure needed for the particular conditions. Just as he must have his fire-box looking like a white-hot jelly at the foot of the long climb up to Shap summit

42. Brighton Locomotive Works of the LBSCR. There is little evidence of any attempt at 'planned layout' and everything appears to be gas-lit, probably with only the bare fish-tail flame. The only power visible is the belt drive from the overhead shafting; otherwise skilled men with hand tools predominate.

so it would be a waste of fuel for the engine to enter Carlisle station afterwards with steam blowing off.

Ideally a good driver and fireman would have worked always together but this could not be guaranteed and inevitably personalities affected the relationship. Many drivers earned the total loyalty and respect of their younger colleagues on the footplate and would teach them all they could about handling the actual driving. They would work the engine economically without waste of fuel and steam, considerate of a fireman's muscles and giving him an occasional breather after a heavy spell. Others thrashed their engines along unfeelingly, using up more coal than necessary, giving their mate harder work and sometimes without a friendly word during the whole trip yet all too ready with criticism, with or without justification.

Most locomotive cabs gave but a minimum of shelter and before 1914 the NER was one of the very few lines to build engines with cabs deep enough to need side windows; in rainy weather countless numbers of enginemen got much wetter than they need have done. Still, it was work to be proud of in its day and even now the older electric or diesel locomotive driver in his neat white overalls and with clean hands has been heard to say a little regretfully, 'The job's not what it was!'

Though earning somewhat less, the goods driver required special skills to start his loose-coupled train of wagons very gently and not to risk so sharp a pull on the rear ones as to break a coupling. There was usually about twenty inches of 'slack' between each truck and similarly the driver had to begin his braking very gradually, starting that 'ting-tong-ting-tong' of the buffers long before the stopping-point. It was also vital for the goods guard to apply the hand brake in his van at the same time. Frequently sparks were to be seen coming from its locked wheels as they skidded along the track. It was a crude way to run trains, depending again upon much human know-how. At steep downhill gradients, notably on the GWR, there were frequently notices at the line-side warning engine crews that 'mineral' trains must be stopped for the hand brakes to be pinned down on a number of the trucks before the descent began; then, when it was over, the train had to stop again for the brakes to be taken off by hand. Another remarkable feature was the great number of privately owned goods wagons, notably those of collieries, which all had to be 'returned empty' to their starting-point.

Signalmen, who came about mid-way down the scale of railway pay, carried great responsibilities in a seemingly tedious job where the consequences of human error could be utter disaster. They too worked their twelve-hour day – often more – and it was a tired man alone in a busy signal-box on a wild night at Hawes Junction up in the Pennines who, in 1910, forgot the presence on the Midland main line of the two light engines into which he unwittingly let the double-headed midnight express from St Pancras run at high speed. When Signalman Sutton saw the low-hanging clouds to his north turn to an angry red in the distance, he realised his terrible mistake and one can faintly imagine his feelings when he asked the man who came to relieve him at 6 a.m.: 'Will you go to Stationmaster Bence and say I am afraid I have wrecked the Scotch express.' In the collision and the fire resulting from the burst gas cylinders below the wooden coaches twelve passengers were killed, some burnt beyond all recognition. This terrible affair is recalled only because it highlights so many of the added

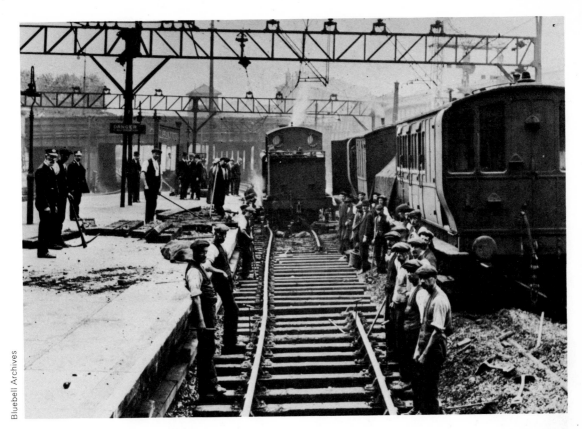

43. Hard labour at Clapham Junction after some minor mishap in which the tank engine has been de-railed; the hand-worked screw jack just below it appears to be the chief means of re-railing since the overhead electric wires could make the use of a crane difficult. All track repairs are being done by hand.

complexities of railway working for *staff* before introduction of the safety measures which are commonplace today. First, the under-powered little engines, of which the MR still used so many, needed piloting up to the Ais Gill summit of the Settle and Carlisle line; this meant that at busy times several of them accumulated at Hawes Junction to be turned and then sent back light to their depots at Carlisle or Leeds. Getting them to the turn-table, then crossed over to their return track and fitted in between slow-moving freight trains and passenger expresses, was obviously a tricky job for the one signalman and on the night in question no fewer than nine such pilot engines had collected owing to extra trains being run before a holiday.

Second, a vital safeguard for signalmen, track-circuiting (which showed up on an electric indicator in the box when a line was occupied) was not then installed at Hawes Junction and the Midland did not use the lever collar, a red object slipped over the signal lever to remind the signalman not to pull it if the line was occupied. (With typical Victorian severity the MR did not believe in

44. The GWR Ocean Mail, some from Canada, probably via Plymouth, arriving at Paddington. To the right is the mail train with its vans and to the left are the horse-drawn carts and vans upon which the mail bags are loaded by hand for conveyance to the GPO. The dim night lighting of an important terminus seems remarkable by today's standards.

them because it could 'foster carelessness in the signalmen'.) Had either of these devices been in use at the time the disaster could scarcely have occurred. It was, of course, made the more ghastly by the fire, which would not have broken out with such savagery (if at all) had all the carriages been electrically lit, as were the sleeping-cars. The burden of long hours and single-handed responsibility was very great for such men as Signalman Sutton.

Shunters were lowly members of the railway army who none the less performed a dangerous and vital job, especially in days when the country's freight moved almost entirely by rail. Their work was to organise the movement of trains, or parts of trains, to the various lines in a marshalling yard for assembly into one main train. The process had also to be done in reverse, to disperse the trucks of an incoming train into separate sections. Latterly sophisticated electronic methods have dispensed with most of the handwork formerly essential in marshalling yards but in earlier times it was largely a matter of loose shunting of individual wagons with the shunter riding precariously on an axle-box, hanging on to the truck with one hand, his shunter's pole held in the other. The shunting engine – often a short-wheelbase 0–6–0 tank engine, pushing the trucks – would give a few sharp puffs, then clap on its brakes and let the truck (or trucks) to be shunted roll on, running over the points into the siding. Before it hit (with a resounding clang) the trucks to which it was to be attached the shunter would jump down and run ahead in order to lift up the crude three-link coupling with his pole and drop it over the hook of the adjoining truck. Similarly, with the pole, he could uncouple other trucks without the dangerous expedient of having to go in between them and risk being crushed by the buffers. At best it was highly dangerous work, particularly in a big marshalling yard where several shunting operations went on at the same time, and one false step or a moment of forgetfulness might mean death or at least the loss of a limb.

Platelayers, those who worked on the permanent way, were others who performed hard and dangerous railway work. Today the Civil Engineers are usually given 'total occupancy' of the track at night or over a weekend for relaying and extensive repairs but formerly the work was done during the day – when overtime rates did not have to be paid – and signs were put beside the line to warn drivers of speed restrictions and the platelayers had to look out for themselves. Not until the Railway Servants Prevention of Accidents Act in 1900 was there adequate provision for look-out men always to be on duty, and among the usual notices to passengers in the compartments was 'Do not throw out of the window anything likely to injure the men working on the line'. The *Railway Magazine* of 1909 complimented the LSWR upon having settled amicably the claim of their permanent way men for an increase in wages. The terms of the award have a certain period interest: actual amounts of the increases varied from sixpence to one shilling (from $2\frac{1}{2}$p to 5p) per week, applying only to those who had been employed on track work for not less than four years, and it did 'not apply to extra workmen, flagmen or watchmen and the Company reserves the right to increase or decrease the amounts in their uncontrolled judgement if circumstances should demand such variation'. However, the money must be seen as worth at least twenty times what it would be today.

Mention of platelayers would not be complete without reference to another and often unpleasant part of their job, that of fogmen.

Fifty years before our Clean Air Act, when the open coal fire was the standard form of house heating and all railways depended upon the coal-fired steam locomotive, dense fogs were frequent. In cities they were at their worst, with the Thames Valley approaches to London representing, probably, the most difficult of all conditions for railway working. Many times in an average winter visibility would be reduced to a very few yards, making it totally impossible for the old semaphore signals or their oil lamps to be picked out by an engine driver until he had run right up to them. On busy lines trains could not be run at normal speeds but some assistance was given to drivers by the placing of fog signals on the line where there could be distant signals at danger. The resultant explosion gave warning that speed must be reduced because the next signal would be at danger. Experienced platelayers were at such times inevitably taken off their work on the permanent way and had to spend their time beside a signal, or signals, setting the detonators on the line when necessary. They were at least provided with a little hut like a sentry box and a coke brazier. In a bad winter as many as 2 million fog signals might be detonated on English railways.

All in all it is not surprising that, in a highly competitive age when labour was plentiful and cheap and managements were under constant pressure to economise in order to maintain their dividends, railway work was found to be third on the list of dangerous occupations, exceeded only by mining and merchant seafaring. Yet in its day it never lacked recruits who went on to take great pride in their job.

5
Stations and Signals

To a railway lover most stations had their attractions especially when they represent-ed the real gateway to the outer world, the point through which came and went people, animals and merchandise. The station for a small town or village could still show an interesting cross-section of its life and work. Its buildings revealed the quality of traffic: the length of platforms – did long trains, or only locals stop there? Did many signals suggest a nearby junction and trains being switched from one line to another? Was there a good-sized waiting room and a separate one for ladies? Had it a bookstall and perhaps a refreshment room, or at least a buffet? Were there scores of telephone wires on huge posts or were there just a handful on a small post – this indicated nearness to the headquarters of the line, or the reverse. Near London there might be double posts heavily loaded whereas in Cumberland or Devon a main-line station might show fewer than a dozen wires. Unlike those of most other countries our stations had platforms about three feet above ground, enabling the passenger to enter the train usually with no more than one shallow step up – a tremendous advantage by comparison with the steep haul up at least three steep steps obligatory all over Continental Europe.

Architecturally stations deserve more books to themselves and while in recent years, especially since nationalisation, many of the older ones have disappeared, before the First World War railway stations comprised a great number of extremely pleasant and many magnificent early Victorian buildings. Famous terminals like Paddington, or cities such as York on its sweeping curve, still present splen-did examples of bold and courageous use of the new material of cast iron allied with glass. In fact most such stations followed the Crystal Palace, which attracted much attention as a pioneering venture.

Certain of the main lines, notably the LNWR, the Midland and the North Eastern, as well as the Great Western, had a tendency to build massive 'all-over' roofs to their im-portant stations and in most cases this involved a considerable additional height to the struc-ture to allow the steam from the engines to disperse upwards. Many, like Euston or Manchester Piccadilly, rebuilt since electrifi-cation, have dispensed with the earlier covering and one cannot help doubting whether it was ever really necessary; most trains, certainly by the turn of the century, were of such a length that their locomotives would have run beyond the covered part of the platform before drawing to a stop. And so as they started up, producing the maximum amount of exhaust steam and smoke, they would have been out in the open air anyhow. Rather it seems that the great 'all-over' roofs were largely a proud and triumphant gesture of the success of the great new method of travel. Certainly there is evidence all over the country of imposing and well designed stations which were built more handsomely and elaborately than was strictly necessary for their purpose but – like the fine trains which they housed – they enriched their surroundings and the general 'image' of railways.

In Edwardian days the different lines had certain characteristics which marked their stations. The rather pretty gabled style of the glass-roofed platform awnings of the MR has been mentioned and for several companies the cast-iron pillars for such awnings were highly decorated, as were the brackets supporting them. The edges of the awnings, too, were frequently the subject of extraordinarily elaborate fretwork which was supposed to assist the collection and drainage of rain water.

One saw the same idea at work for seaside buildings on pier or esplanade. In this matter of both awnings and pillars the LBSCR was most successful with many of its stations all over Sussex and Surrey. To this day an excellent example is to be found in Sheffield Park station on the Bluebell Line. One stands amazed at the amount of money which could be found by a public company for pure decor-

45. Local stone used to good effect in this mid-Victorian station at Machynlleth in Wales. The engine with its tall chimney emphasises the antiquity of much of the stock still in use in 1909 ; the water column with its circular tank at the platform end is another mark of earlier days.

LCGB (Ken Nunn Collection)

ation over a century ago and at a time when the wealth of the country per head was very much less than it is today. Considerable taste also was in evidence as some companies employed architects who made skilful use of local materials, producing station buildings in the characteristic stones of Devon, the Cotswolds or Derbyshire. Others again, such as the LNWR and the GNR, seemed to concentrate upon one particular type of brick for many of their stations.

A means for passengers to cross the line had always to be provided and it seems strange that, apart from larger stations, it was nearly always the footbridge that was preferred. Doubtless it cost less to build but would have been more expensive in maintenance and probably required passengers to take more steps up and down than did the subway. The bridge

46. Kettering, Northants, is an excellent example of the classic Midland station, well spaced out with its up and down — almost saw-tooth — gabled roofing for the central platform. Note also the ingenious form of angled name-board, enabling it to be legible from some distance down the platform.

was a very fine viewpoint for watching trains, especially if it were mainly of wood and had open sides.

A main-line station was the most rewarding, one where plenty of expresses went tearing through and also where a few important trains stopped, as well as all the local traffic. From the footbridge you could sight a fast train perhaps a mile away, watch the pinpoint grow rapidly, the pure white plume of steam pouring from the funnel of the engine the front of which usually swung slightly from side to side as it traversed the rail joints. Then a hot blast of smoke puffed out under the bridge, some of it shooting up between the boards one stood upon, and from below came the rapid 'doodly-do, doodly-do, doodly-do' as the coach bogies raced over the track and in seconds the train was passed. Then only the fast diminishing end of the last coach was to be seen, its half-vestibule connection swinging from side to side, some waste paper caught up in its wake and a few wreaths of steam. There was nothing to equal the sight and sound of a steam express passing through a station at speed: if you were on the platform there was the shout of 'stand back' from porters as the engine with its flailing side rods came thundering towards you. Its whistle sounded a joyous note which dropped a semitone as it receded and over all, of course, that memorable smell of the steam train.

Platform tickets were unknown before the First World War; on most stations even a boy train watcher was left in peace, and there could be a great deal to see. The part of the platform where engines stopped was of course a favourite viewpoint. The locos with outside cylinders, say a GWR 4-6-0, a GNR Atlantic or a Midland Compound, were the most interesting because you could follow the motion of piston and slide valve, moving in perfect harmony with the driving wheels as they came slowly to rest, with gobbets of oil and usually spots of hot water on them. You might even see the ordinary bottle corks which some engines had stuck into the top of their lubricating points.

One could tell whether the boiler was at full pressure with steam blowing off through the safety valves and, perhaps, the sound of the engine would change as the fireman applied the injector to bring more cold water into the boiler, thus reducing the pressure temporarily. The moment of starting was al-

ways one to watch: usually it was the fireman who looked out for the wave of the guard's flag, signalled to the driver who perhaps pulled the whistle chain and then gave that sharp thrust on the regulator which produced the immediate change of note in the engine sound and the first movement of the wheels. If the rails were greasy there might be the thrill of a wheel-slip – they made perhaps a whole revolution, even more, without gripping, and there would be the sharp chuff-chuff-chuff from the engine while the fireman at once applied the sanding gear and the driver immediately reduced the regulator opening. Probably at the next cautious opening the engine would get away but sometimes it needed coaxing gently off with two or three separate openings and shuttings. When that happened there were creaks and clonks from the couplings as buffers were alternately extended and compressed; the train would seem to complain audibly. Several sharp puffs in succession could wreak havoc with the fire, pulling holes in it which the fireman then had to fill up as quickly as possible. To thrash the engine at such a point – as I once saw a French driver do when he stuck on the sharp curve into the Harbour station at Dieppe – could be bad for the track though enormously imposing as a demonstration of steam power! The black exhaust smoke shot up with a thunderous roar from the great locomotive as her wheels spun for some seconds while she remained motion-

British Rail

British Rail

British Rail

48 (left). Paddington arrival platform, Christmas 1908. Under Brunel's neatly symmetrical roof there stands a large accumulation of the famous metal milk churns whose clangs resounded on every station. Horse cabs are drawn up on the far side of the platform.

49 (above). The bookstall on the departure platform at Paddington pre-1914 presents a very different aspect from to-day, with its travelling rugs and Ingersoll watches. While the expensive 'glossies' predominate among the periodicals, there is a display of the then popular 'Sevenpenny Copyright' books, and cigars and cigarettes also compete for space.

less then, at last, the train heaved forward to its resting-place beside the waiting steamer.

Any station where trains were divided and coaches detached had its special rewards for the watcher. Porters dropped nimbly on to the track, slipped between the coach ends, turned off the taps of vacuum brake and heating pipes, then disconnected them and tucked the loose ends on to their holders. Next the slackening off of the screw coupling – upon which the comfort of the starting and stopping of all passenger coaches was dependent – unhooking its great weight from the adjoining coach and banging it neatly on to the spare hook of its own vehicle. Then the porter would wriggle his way back on to the platform, put the red rear-end lamp on the last coach of the train and signal to the guard that the job was done. Meanwhile a shunting engine would come cautiously along to deal with the detached coach, perhaps removing it to a siding or pushing it on to a train in another platform.

At many lesser stations the shunting of one or two vans or trucks might be done by a couple of cart-horses in tandem. They could pull straight ahead, stepping across the sleepers in the 'four-foot way' between the rails, or sometimes they were hooked on to the side of the vehicle, themselves proceeding in the 'six-foot way' between two sets of tracks but able to let the truck run on independently to make the required contact with the train or the other trucks they were to join. It was quite a comfortable job for horses accustomed to the sound of engines; they never appeared over-driven, their hooves got a firm grip on the rough surface of the ballast, they had seemingly just to lean their weight against the collar and with one heave the truck would start to roll. The operation normally proceeded at walking pace and at the cost then of horse-feed and labour it was doubtless cheaper than main-taining an engine in steam all day.

A horse unused to railways, and handled by those with whom it was not familiar, could create terrible scenes when urged to enter the horse-box. As many as five men might attempt to pull at its bridle, crack whips at its sides and use a broomhead pressed flat against its hindquarters. Still worse was the mournful trail of cattle goaded up the special white-washed loading dock to be rammed into the cattle trucks, which were roofed but with open sides. Rail was then, of course, the essential mode of transport for meat on the hoof and it is at least arguable that it was less uncom-fortable than the swaying, swerving road vehicle.

Mention of cattle leads to the enormous milk traffic of railways always in evidence at stations. The LSWR alone brought a huge gallonage into London every morning from the rich pasturelands of Dorset and Devon and certain platforms at Waterloo used to smell of sour milk for most of the day (even so, it was said in the *Railway Magazine* of 1908 that it amounted to no more than one half pint a day for 500,000 people for 'the poor use milk in very small quantities'). Nevertheless, the coming of railways transformed the avail-ability of fresh milk in cities here and their readiness to convey it at specially cheap rates put English town dwellers in a better position than those of most Continental countries. Thus the great conical-shaped metal milk churns were a regular part of the station scene. They were of such a weight that it would take two men to unload the full churn from a van but once it was on the platform a single man could propel it merely by holding the large knob in the centre of its lid. He would let the churn revolve on the edge of its circular base, the whole leaning at an angle of about 70° to the ground. Every porter seemed to possess the knack of performing this feat safely, in-cluding the art of letting go of the churn at precisely the right moment to ensure that it rolled to rest with a clang, standing upright beside its brethren. Only once did I ever see a misjudgement result in a great gush of milk from a fallen churn which then took two men to right it. The clatter of those milk churns was inseparable from railway stations, suggestive of cheerful bustle by day but strangely mournful in the small hours of a night journey.

Years before the advent of electric signalling the working of signals and points was a prominent feature of the station scene. Every station had, usually visible from the platform, the Home signal controlling the entry of the train into the platform and the Starter at the far end to send it on its journey after the stop. The Distant signal might be seen some hun-dreds of yards before the station and possibly the Advance Starter equally far ahead.

Signal posts and gantries could be works of art and many lines had their own character-istics in matters of detail, although before 1914 there was no nonsense about 'upper quadrant'

National Railway Museum

50. The main cab yard at the old Waterloo station. The hansom cab was still popular up to 1910 and after, but the four-wheeler or 'growler' performed the hard work as can be deduced from the one to the left of the photo: trunks on the roof, sometimes an extra one on the box beside the driver and possibly a total of five adults in all was a terrible load for one horse, especially up the steep incline to the high-level tracks at Waterloo. Extra refinement provides a second-class waiting room for ladies. The departure board on the left shows the interesting range of destinations.

Bluebell Archives

51 (above). Signal complexities. The approach to Brighton station, LBSCR, where economy in the use of posts, with both incoming and departure signals on the same one, must have added to a driver's problems and the risks of misunderstanding.

52 (below). An imposing group of signals on the GWR at Royal Oak. Each one bears a message for the approaching driver whether ML, indicating that his train remains on the main line, or RL, meaning a cross-over to be taken to the relief line, etc. Meanwhile the two-cylinder 4–6–0 'Lady of the Lake' strides out with a train showing the changing colour of the carriage livery, some in the original 'chocolate and cream', other coaches in the later Edwardian crimson lake.

Ian Allan Collection

positions. All signals when 'off' went down into the lower quadrant. To say that the train 'was signalled' was synonymous with its being 'down' but there were still variations between the lines. The Great Western, with its usual individuality, had signals different from those of any other line, they dropped down more sharply, to make an acute angle with the signal post – 30° whereas the normal was about 45°. It gave their signals an exceedingly 'high speed' look which was possibly the intention! Another variation was the curious and altogether unique 'somersault' signal used by the GNR. With this type the arm was pivoted in the centre of the blade and when it went 'down' into the 'off' position it dropped to a steep angle and quite clear of the post. To the uninitiated it seemed to be falling right off the post but it appeared to answer satisfactorily. The Midland on the other hand gave the impression of dropping to slightly less than the normal 45°. Their speciality was a long sharp spike on top of their wooden signal posts and instead of the white band across the red arm of the signal they used a white spot, as did also the SE & CR. Most railways used the wooden post on which to mount the arm but some, including the LSWR and some Scottish lines, preferred the steel lattice type.

At any kind of junction, especially one with up to four tracks, mechanical signalling – as distinct from electric light signals – called for elaborate gantries of which, perhaps, the most famous was that for the LNWR main line at Rugby where trains from the South could approach on any one of three running lines and from each a train could be sent through or into Rugby in three different ways. Allowing for Home and Distant signals on each post there was a total of twenty-two arms and, because they had to be duplicated at high and low levels, it amounted in all to a total of forty-four signal arms. One realises the perfection of eyesight demanded of drivers who were to pick out their signals correctly from the dim oil lights on a misty night with engine steam blowing about and when they were themselves approaching at speed. The mind boggles also at the intricate work of the signal engineers who correctly fitted and maintained the maze of wires, pulleys and points rods controlled by the forest of levers in the old manually worked signal-box.

The track circuit, which indicated electrically in the signal-box the presence of a train on a given line, did not come into general use until well into the 1900s and it was 1906 before the GWR experimented with its 'audible warning', which sounded in the driver's cab when a distant signal was passed at danger. Edwardian journeys lacked a great many of the now standard safeguards.

To return, however, to the station platform, there was greater variety of entertainment than we know today. It seemed to be profitable to keep an astonishing number of slot machines supplied with articles which were all sold for a penny: bars of plain and of milk chocolate, different biscuits (some with 'cream' in them, usually rather sour), sweets, boxes of matches. On one machine was the picture of an alluring gypsy lady below the inscription: 'To tell you your fortune I do not pretend but I'll give you some fun if a penny you'll spend.' The weight of the coin caused her to spin round until her finger came to rest pointing to the legend conveying some romantic fate.

Besides the great enamelled tin advertisements there were the quite attractive appeals from the individual railways to travel upon their lines: colourful posters of the LNWR of ships from Holyhead for Ireland, the GNR for Skegness, the LSWR was 'the path to the sun' – Bournemouth in particular – and the

GWR for South Devon and Cornwall. Thomas Cook showed their extraordinary moustachioed giant flying with a magic carpet outspread on his back on which were grouped relaxed and delighted tourists looking down upon the Alps.

Station refreshment rooms, though having a reputation for stale sandwiches, could produce good pots of tea and that at Yeovil Junction on the LSWR stands out in memory. My father, coming home from a Cornish holiday with his brood of five children, was disappointed – my mother still more so – to find that no restaurant car was added to their afternoon train at Exeter as had been expected. A ticket inspector, learning of the problem, at once undertook to telegraph to Yeovil fifty miles ahead for tea baskets. He was as good as his word and, as the train drew into the station, there, outside the refreshment room, anxiously scanning the incoming carriages, was a man with four flat baskets in his arms – three doubles and a single. A pot of fresh-made tea in one little compartment, milk, bread and butter, madeira cake and jam in others, and all for one shilling a head. Each basket had a large enamel label 'Yeovil Junction' to which it was returned after being put out at Salisbury, the next major station; it was all a most neat and tidy arrangement and typical of the times, if unworkable today.

The Midland, which looked after its passengers' comfort particularly well, offered 'Luncheon Baskets' for three shillings (15p) containing 'Half a chicken and ham or tongue, salad, bread, cheese and butter etc.' with half a bottle of claret or burgundy. There was also a cheaper one for two shillings containing 'Veal and ham pie, salad, cheese, bread, etc.' and a bottle of stout.

As yet further compensation before steam heating of carriages was general, the MR also provided very handsome foot-warmers encased in thick carpet-like material and with a brass handle at one end. A humorous drawing of the period showed a loving couple sitting very close in the train with no fewer than five such articles to complete their comfort, feet on one, behinds on another, a third across their knees and others in the small of the back and at the shoulders. The wise man never travelled any distance in winter without a thick overcoat and a rug. If he were fortunate he might even possess a 'Railway Companion' – a neatly fitted container for a sandwich box and a flask as well as the small candle or oil reading-lamp so valuable in the dimly lit compartments before gas or electric lighting was general.

Official notices on and about stations of seventy years ago included the famous one of the SE & CR at Charing Cross: 'Any cabman skylarking or otherwise misconducting himself while on the Managing Committee's premises or Smoking whilst his cab is standing alongside the Platform will be required to leave the Station immediately.'

The Cheshire Lines also were peremptory with cabmen (and others): 'These closets are intended for the convenience of passengers only, workmen, cabmen, fishporters and idlers are not permitted to use them.'

In days of the loose-coupled goods trains with no continuous braking system one might find, on a station at the top of a long uphill gradient, 'Train Arrived Complete Bell' – to be rung to indicate to the signalman that the incoming goods train was all in one piece.

A gem of steam days was: 'NOTICE TO ENGINEMEN OF DOWN THROUGH STOPPING TRAINS – Train to be brought to a stand so that engine does not pass this board.' Its purpose was to avoid the chance of steam from the engine's safety valves obscuring the

53. The approach to the rather untidy jumble of
LSWR platforms at the old Waterloo prior to its
complete re-building in the early 1900s. Here again is
the potentially confusing use of the same post for
signals indicating both arrivals and departures. The
former signals have on their arms the number of the
platform which they control: the smaller arms
below are for the movement of light engines (which
had to stop at that point after they had helped out a
train by pushing from the rear). Incidentally, the
second engine from the left has on its buffer beam
the unusual disc with the black centre indicating
that it is a 'Special' – in this case for Southampton
Docks.

view of the signalman in the busy box at the end of the island platform immediately above where the engine would normally stand if it overran the platform slightly. One was puzzled as to how any driver could see and take in the meaning of the rather complicated notice until his engine had already reached the point where it could not be stopped in time!

'Chorclicks, cigarettes, pap*ers*' was a standard chant sung out at every station of importance by the newsagents' boys who patrolled the platform beside a standing train, their wicker trays filled with the aforesaid merchandise. They wore smart peaked caps bearing the name of the newsagents who employed them, W. H. Smith, Wymans or Menzies, according to the part of the country and the particular line involved. The former had the concession for most railway companies, Wymans the LNWR and GWR, while Scotland was covered by John Menzies of Edinburgh.

Lastly, the wheel-tapper made his presence known at stations – at least to passengers on an express when it stopped at an important place. Armed with his lamp and the hammer with a handle about three feet long, he usually strode along the 'six-foot way' between the running tracks and with a deft swing and turn of his wrist he cracked his hammer on the rim of each wheel to make sure that it emitted the right sound – a rather high pitched tonk. If the note were flat it could indicate a cracked wheel. Then it was a case of 'all out' and the coach was taken out of the train, leaving the unfortunate passengers to find seats elsewhere if they could. The wheel-tapper also felt each axle-box with the back of his hand to make sure it had not run hot, and flashed his lamp at the couplings; on the one side of a train of ten coaches he had forty wheels to check and more, if some of them were dining- or sleeping-cars with six-wheel bogies. Modern metallurgy has made him redundant but, like so many other humble railway servants, he made his vital contribution to safety in the past.

6
Comforts and Curiosities

Of Queen Victoria's reign it has been said that there was no greater development in social well-being than that offered by railways; in King Edward's time it reached its zenith, in comfort and convenience, for those who could afford to travel. For the middle classes, at least, there was a level of personal attention which leaves one amazed today. One writer in the *Railway Magazine* of the time referred, for example, to the 'dignified and quietly polite bearing of the LNWR Guard who, with stately courtesy, shows a party of distinguished travellers to the First Class or, with fatherly care lifts some poor woman's child into a Third Class compartment' – all this preparatory to swinging himself gracefully on to the footboard of the moving train after he had waved the 'right away' with his green flag.

On some lines each compartment in a corridor train had a bell-push by which one could summon a waiter. The bell indicator in the dining-car probably did no more than show from which coach the summons had issued and the waiter had to look inquiringly into each of its six or seven compartments before he could identify his customer. Still, the system worked with the shorter trains before 1914. The LSWR also obliged with a long narrow table which was made to fit between the seats of the side-corridor compartment, and on which meals could be served. Two or three of them were always to be found folded and strapped together at the end of the corridor; the compartment table system continued with the Southern right up to the electric expresses of the 1960s but the compartment bell-pushes had long since been removed.

When the railways adopted corridor trains and dining-cars they were lavish in providing for the hunger and thirst of the comparatively small numbers travelling. Some Midland expresses drawn by one of Samuel Johnson's most elegant 4–2–2 Single Drivers – quite capable of gliding downhill at 90 mph – consisted of only five bogie coaches, of which one was a sumptuous twelve-wheeled dining-car. The Great Central in direct competition with the MR over part of the former's 'London Extension' offered exactly the same proportion of refreshment cheer in its five-coach 'fliers'. At another level the LNWR surpassed all others in the luxury of the special stock, built in 1908, for their American boat trains between Liverpool Riverside Station and Euston. This was before the full development of Southampton Docks had enabled the LSWR to inveigle the Cunard, White Star and other lines to use that port in place of Liverpool.

British Rail

54 (above).   Tables laid for a four-course lunch in a GWR restaurant car of 1906 and flowers on each show great confidence in the expectations of smooth running. It is lit by elaborate brass 'electroliers' in the roof and the curtains in the gangway divide smoking from the non-smoking sections. The provision of separate chairs saved some space but did not give quite so solid a ride as fixed seating.

55 (right).   LNWR family saloon for day travel and clearly furnished to first-class standards. Father and mother presumably occupied the two end seats with their anti-macassars while children might sprawl on the sofa and nurse or governess sit in the wicker chair opposite. At one end of the coach would be a compartment for maids and at the other a lavatory and luggage accommodation.

Nothing was too good for the richest visitors to England and, as the colour 'pull-out' frontispiece of the *Railway Magazine* showed, the gorgeous train of ten vehicles carried two dining-cars to satisfy the passengers in only six coaches; the other two were luggage vans essential to convey the huge wardrobe trunks without which no well-dressed lady could cross the Atlantic then. It is said that Americans were invariably impressed by the gentle starting of that train and the miraculous smoothness of the track of the 'Premier Line' – both very different from the rougher riding on their own railways, despite the all-steel

Pullmans. (As an aside, after the disaster to the LSWR American Boat Express from Plymouth the New York press had some hard things to say about the light construction of our wooden rolling stock but it was a fact that greater care in working and track maintenance, then, in Britain resulted in proportionately fewer fatal accidents here.)

Another great boon for the few was the system of the Club Carriage developed most successfully in the north. This was a comfortable saloon which could be used only by the club members and it had, needless to say, its own bar and steward in attendance. The

LNWR ran one from Blackpool to Manchester; the Lancashire and Yorkshire was also in the business; and the Midland was one of the most enterprising with a Morecambe to Bradford and Leeds Club Carriage involving a daily run of sixty miles in each direction. Assuming it was mainly or exclusively first class it is difficult to see how it could have paid the railways as there was a strictly limited number of customers to buy the drinks and the coach itself must have had little, if any, chance of alternative use apart from its morning and evening run. Nevertheless it was yet one more example of the comfortable service offered by railways and extremely pleasant for gregarious commuters who did not necessarily seek quiet respite at the start and end of their day!

At the lower end of the income scale railways were of enormous benefit to workmen, offering cheap early morning fares to enable them to live in the inner suburbs though working in London. The Great Eastern suburban train with its six-a-side four-wheel coach and hard wooden seats might seem a poor thing compared, for example, with the neat 'bogie blocks' – four-coach sets steam heated, electrically lit and well upholstered – of the LSWR, but the former carried its humble traveller by early Workmen's Train five miles to work and back for 2d ('tuppence', which was less than half of 2p today) giving ten miles of travel in all. To be fair to the South Western it must be said that up to the 1914 War they gave twenty-four miles for their sevenpenny workmen's ticket, including the return journey. There the impecunious breadwinners, or mothers with children bent upon a cheap 'day in Town' could travel in the six-wheel stock normally kept for the 'Race Specials' to Sandown Park, Esher. Later some of those same carriages were to be cut up and put on new underframes to become bogie stock for the first of the South Western Electrics, originally nicknamed Green Caterpillars.

Some twenty years before England knew Austin Seven motor cars, railway day excursions were enormously popular, especially at Bank Holidays. Seaside resorts were the most sought-after destinations, notably Blackpool in the north and Brighton and Bournemouth in the south, and fares would often be less than a third of the normal 'penny a mile' of the third-class rate. Thus one might take a day return trip from Waterloo to Bournemouth, 216 miles of travel in all, for five shillings (25p). Up to about 1900 the oldest stock of comfortless four-wheelers might be reserved for excursionists, and not without reason because some of them had disagreeable personal habits, but as time went on good bogie coaches were run on such trains which were timed at express speeds. Normally, excursion trains were composed of only third-class though the inclusion of an occasional composite coach challenged the tripper to take a chance and ride 'first' with a strong likelihood that he would get away with it. However, in 1909 the plea was made, again in the *Railway Magazine*: 'Why not first class excursions? There are many well bred who cannot afford 1st class [normally] and those suffering from love's young dreams who would gladly pay more – on an excursion – for more exclusive accommodation.'

Bank Holiday traffic was big business for many railways and it was a real service, conferring great benefits upon working men and their families in days before even the annual week or ten days paid holiday was general. The GWR offered an all-time record in 1909 with a day trip from Paddington to Newton Abbot, a non-stop run of 192 miles, while the LSWR produced a considerable feat of or-

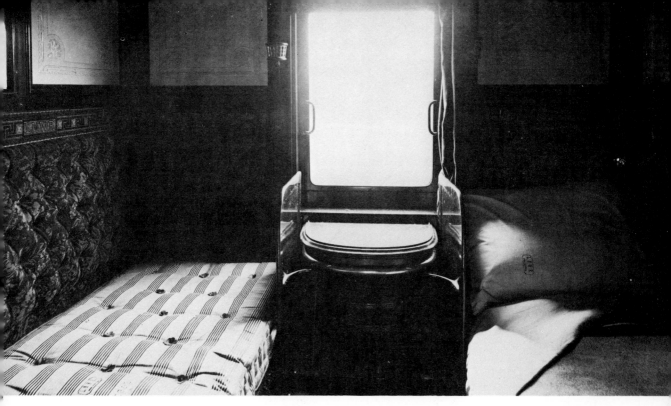

56. A spacious double first-class sleeper on the
West Coast route seventy years ago (there were
none for third class then). Beds of reasonable width
were provided and were well protected from
unwelcome splashes from the basin but there is
curious lack of all those bedside lights and useful
racks and shelves so handy in modern sleepers.

ganisation, in steam days, with an Easter
Monday half-hourly service from Waterloo to
Bournemouth non-stop in two hours ten
minutes. It ran from 1.20 p.m. to 8.20 p.m.
and is mentioned only to emphasise the lengths
to which railways would go in search of extra
traffic as well as the astonishing level of service
provided for the travelling public. It was a
remarkable achievement of the Waterloo
operating department to produce all the extra
carriages required over and above the usual
timetable and the additional engines in steam
with the essential number of top-link crews
to man them. Many must have worked long
hours on that day.

In Edwardian times the special train – as in
the days of Sherlock Holmes – was still the
way *par excellence* by which the wealthy man
in a hurry could dash about the country. It
was to be had usually for 7s 6d (37½p) a mile

with a minimum charge of £5 and for the
American tycoon – for example – who missed
the boat train at Waterloo and the chance of
sailing in the *Mauretania* to cross in five days,
the special was definitely a proposition. After
all, what was £25 when the alternative was a
delay of several days? Provided the line was
clear a Drummond T9 Greyhound or an
Adams 4–4–0 with but a couple of coaches
behind the tender could average 60 mph with
no difficulty and run at well over 80 in places.
To see the short train tearing along – the
special locomotive head code displayed either
by lamp or disc arrangement – was always an

British Rail

57. Officially described as 'Tea Compartment', this apparatus was provided at the end of a sleeping car and enabled the attendant to brew up tea or coffee to revive travellers after the night journey. It might also have provided heating for the entire vehicle.

excitement and one longed to know where it was going and who was in it.

Anyone who saw the famous documentary film, *Night Mail*, knows the peculiar romance of the 8.30 p.m. Postal Special from Euston with its team of London sorters working away in the mail vans through the night until the train reached Carlisle where they were replaced by Scots. Merely to see it standing in the platform at Euston had a sense of drama, with the 'T.P.O.' – Travelling Post Office – vans, their folded nets held firmly against the side of the coach, ready to be extended to catch mail bags, and the powerful lights at footboard level to assist in the dropping of other bags from the train, all to be done at full speed. Then there was that neatly painted reproduction of the Royal Arms above the

little letter-box on the coach side and the note informing you that letters posted in that box must bear an extra ½d stamp. Whether anyone took advantage of it at Carlisle in the small hours seems doubtful but for urgent matters of business to post on the train at Crewe in the late evening might be well worthwhile. Moreover, the odd mail van was to be found on many an express in the daytime and at its stops that special posting facility had its uses.

The many separate railways serving London before the 1914 war made their presence felt in the streets by the number of well turned

58. The TPO, or Travelling Post Office, of the West Coast Joint Stock (LNWR and CR), in which the mails could be sorted at night while the train went on its way. The incandescent gas burners gave a brilliant light to help sorters in their work.

out horse-drawn vans that were to be seen. They each bore the initials of their railway owners and many carried some hint of the colours of the line. The GWR, for example, had the van bodies painted in their chocolate-brown and the Midland, inevitably, sported their famous crimson lake. There were also horse buses maintained by the railways which provided an invaluable service between terminals such as King's Cross, Waterloo, Victoria and Paddington, which saved many a family the expense of a cab. The buses were single-deckers which nevertheless accommodated plenty of luggage on their roofs.

Associated with this in some measure is the rather terrible memory of what could be seen by many a family which did hire a cab at, say, Euston or Liverpool Street to take them direct to their London home, perhaps in Hampstead or Clapham Common. As they drove through one of the poorer districts on the way a ragged man would spot the loaded cab and run behind it – for some miles if need be – solely in the hope of earning sixpence or a shilling by helping to unload the luggage when the party reached home. Then to carry it up a flight of steps from the street – inevitable with a basement house – and perhaps up to the first floor bedrooms was no light task. The desperation of men prepared to put forth such physical effort for so small a reward tells its own story. It was said that the 'runner' needed, beside his fleetness of foot, the judgement at once to assess the precise standing of the family by the quality of their luggage: if it were best quality they were likely to have a manservant who would shun his assistance, and if too shabby the family would expect to handle the luggage themselves – solid respectability with young children was the best prospect! Part of the reverse of the medal which gave such comfort and ease to

the middle classes of Edwardian days is not pleasant to contemplate.

This miscellany of comforts, curiosities and special services offered by railways long ago cannot end without recalling once more the extraordinary attraction which the independent railways exercised upon so many different people – mainly men, it must be admitted. 'Watching trains' might be frowned upon by some ambitious parents as a waste of time ('you should be doing something more useful') but as years went by an Edwardian boy could learn that he was not alone, that scores of men shared his obsession; that on the bridge over Crewe station, for example, or on the fine semicircular platform at York might be found, at certain times, many highly intelligent gentlemen – schoolmasters, clergymen and organists among them – who were completely happy to spend a holiday morning at that deeply absorbing and harmless occupation.

The *aficionado* would know his timetable and which trains were on time, or late. The general appearance of the train, its engine and the coaches of which it was composed would probably identify it and on some lines such as the LSWR or LBSCR the disc code on the front of the engine indicated its precise route. At the great junctions there was always the fun on seeing the trains of a 'foreign' line, one different from that which served one's home town. That almost certainly meant engines and carriages of a different colour, shape and design. Carlisle was another famous point for the keen observer because at that frontier station six great railways came together, LNWR, MR, NER from England and the Caledonian, NBR and GSWR from Scotland, plus the little Maryport and Carlisle. With each line having its pronounced characteristics and a pride in the cleanliness of its stock the galaxy of colours was impressive: shining black North Western, crimson Midland, lightish-green North Eastern, Prussian blue Caledonian, brownish-green North British, to mention only the engines. In the South there was, of course, nothing to equal Carlisle but GWR, LSWR, Midland and South Western, and Somerset and Dorset came together at various junctions such as Salisbury and Templecombe to present their contrast and to give their supporters opportunity to compare and criticise.

Above all, those earlier days of the steam-dominated railways gave unrivalled pleasure to those who cared for 'trains', whether it was the sight of the hard-pounding, bright, clean engine bursting out from under a bridge or a tunnel with its clouds of white steam billowing upwards and trailing along behind it, eventually rolling to one side as it dispersed, and the roar and rhythmical clatter as the train swept by, or again the engine at rest, simmering at the journey's end. At the buffer stops in Paddington a GWR Saint or Star 4-6-0 with its smiling copper-capped chimney could look enormously impressive, plainly satisfied with itself after lifting three or four hundred tons across five counties from Devonshire to London. Equally the Midland Compound 4-4-0 in the arrival platform at St Pancras, though a smaller engine, was something of unforgettable beauty and it had rushed its immaculate train of crimson lake carriages from the dirt of Manchester through the grandeur of the Derbyshire Peak District, then the Leicestershire pastures to end under the great arched roof of the London terminus.

Edwardian trains, like the great sailing ships, were costly and exacting in human labour, but to travel in them had its magnificence and it is good to remember their finest qualities.

59. SECR Stewarts Lane goods yard in South London, where a steam traction engine was the most up-to-date form of road transport, all else being horse-drawn. Once again the amount of hand labour involved is immense: the modern note in that Edwardian scene is the overhead wiring in the background serving the electrified section of the LBSCR.

Bibliography

Allen, P. C. and Macleod, A. B., *Rails in the Isle of Wight*, 1967.
Bagwell, P. S., *The Railwaymen*, 1963.
Ellis, C. Hamilton, *The Trains We Loved*, 1947.
Railway Carriages in the British Isles, 1965.
Hamilton, J. A. B., *Railway Accidents in the 20th Century*, 1967.
Lloyd, Roger, *The Fascination of Railways*, 1952.
Nock, O. S., *British Steam Locomotives*, 1964.
Steam Railways of Britain, 1967.
Tuplin, W. A. *Great Western Steam*, 1958.
North Western Steam, 1963.

INDEX

(References in italic are to photograph page numbers)

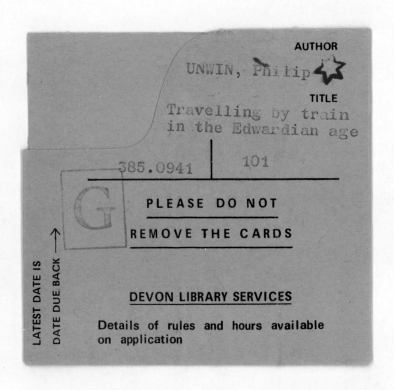